THE FILMS OF
CECIL B. DeMILLE

by GENE RINGGOLD and DeWITT BODEEN

THE FILMS OF

CECIL B. DeMILLE

THE CITADEL PRESS   *Secaucus, New Jersey*

PHOTOGRAPHIC ACKNOWLEDGEMENTS

The Academy of Motion Picture Arts and Sciences; the Estate of Cecil B. DeMille; DeWitt Bodeen; Milton Luboviski; Metro-Goldwyn-Mayer, Inc.; Paramount Pictures, Inc.; and Gene Ringgold.

And special thanks to Miss Lillian Schwartz and her staff at the Motion Picture Academy Library and to Miss Florence Cole, curator and secretary of the DeMille Estate.

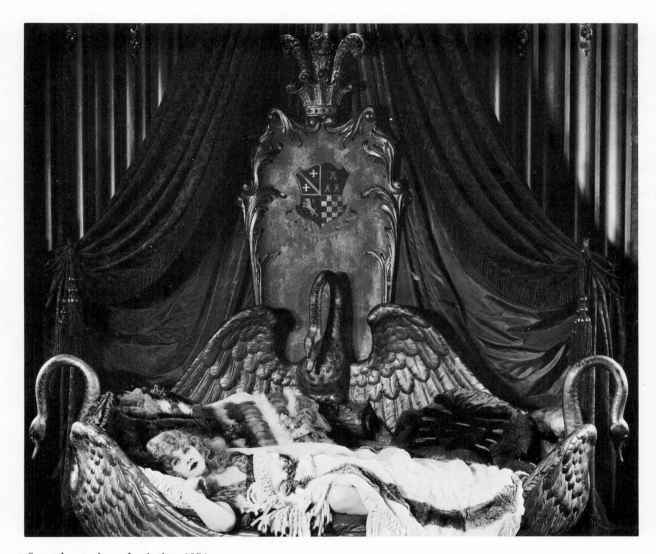

Second paperbound printing, 1974
Copyright © 1969 by Gene Ringgold and DeWitt Bodeen
All rights reserved
Published by Citadel Press
A division of Lyle Stuart, Inc.
120 Enterprise Ave., Secaucus, N.J. 07094
In Canada: George J. McLeod Limited
73 Bathurst St., Toronto 2B, Ontario
Designed by A. Christopher Simon
Manufactured in the United States of America
ISBN 0-8065-0207-X

CONTENTS

INTRODUCTION

A BIOGRAPHICAL SKETCH

Cecil Blount DeMille was born at Ashfield, Massachusetts, on August 12, 1881, the younger of two sons born to Henry Churchill de Mille* and his wife, Mathilda Beatrice.

Henry de Mille taught English at Columbia University, from which he held a degree; he also preached sermons from the pulpit and wrote plays. The outcome of his association with David Belasco was four successful collaborations: *The Wife; Lord Chumley; The Charity Ball; Men and Women.*

Mrs. de Mille (*née* Samuel), an extraordinary woman, turned the family home into a school for girls after her husband's death in February of 1893. Her efforts were successful enough to enable her to send her elder son, William, to Columbia University, and the younger Cecil to the Pennsylvania Military College. She subsequently formed her own theatrical agency, The DeMille Play Company, which flourished for nearly twenty years. She also wrote a number of stories and plays.

Young Cecil ran away from military college to join the recruits for the Spanish-American War, but being under age, he was rejected. Brother William had turned from an interest in engineering, and was studying for the theater, with hopes of establishing himself as a playwright. When Cecil also manifested an interest in theatrics, his mother, amenable to such tastes, enrolled him as a student at the Academy of Dramatic Arts in New York City. That was in

---

* "DeMille" is the form of the name Cecil B. chose to use in his professional career; in his private life, however, he used the family spelling—"de Mille."

Edward Hoster

the fall of 1898. On February 21, 1900, he made his debut as an actor at New York's Garden Theater, in the Charles Frohman production *Hearts Are Trumps*.

He acted in numerous other productions, and, while on tour with *Hearts Are Trumps*, he met Constance Adams, an actress who had joined the company. She was the daughter of a Boston judge. Cecil DeMille married her on August 16, 1902.

By now William was established as one of the young hopefuls among the new American play-wrights, and Cecil had similar aspirations. He is credited with the idea for Belasco's *The Return of Peter Grimm*, and he collaborated with William on several plays: *The Genius*, *The Royal Mounted*, and *After Five*. None of these vehicles, however, was as successful as William de Mille's solo efforts. Cecil also authored a few plays, but playwriting never became his forte.

But, as general manager of his mother's company, he met many prominent theatrical personalities, and his friendship with a vaudeville musician, Jesse L. Lasky, led to their collaborating

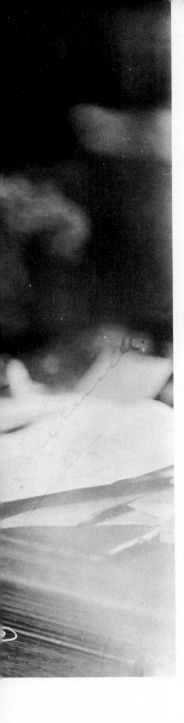

joined them in the project. So did Arthur Friend, a young attorney.

DeMille had no money to invest in the company, but he was named Director-General. Lasky was made head of the organization, Sam Goldfish became the film salesman, and Arthur Friend handled the company's legal affairs. When approached by Cecil about joining the group and investing in the company's future, William de Mille rejected the whole project. He was enjoying his first years of genuine recognition as a playwright and could not then see any future in the motion picture world.

The newly-formed company purchased the film rights to Edwin Milton Royle's successful play, *The Squaw Man*, and Dustin Farnum was signed to play the title role for a salary of $250 a week. The young producers tried to interest Farnum in accepting the quarter interest in the company which William de Mille had scorned, but Farnum wanted the cash.

It was decided to shoot *The Squaw Man* in Arizona, although the actual locale of the story was Wyoming. None of the producers had actually seen very much of the West, but in their minds Arizona typified the Far West. Accordingly, five of those concerned set forth together for Flagstaff, Arizona: Director-General De-Mille; Oscar C. Apfel, a film director who had some experience in Eastern studios; Albert Gandolfi, a cameraman; Dustin Farnum; and Fred Kley, Farnum's secretary and dresser.

As their train moved west, DeMille and Apfel worked on the scenario they intended to use, based on an adaptation that author Royle had prepared. But when they reached Flagstaff they discovered that that part of Arizona was not the West they had envisaged. DeMille knew that at the end of the railroad line lay Los Angeles, where other film makers, including D. W. Griffith, were producing successful films, even during the winter months. The five men came to a quick decision: They got back on the train and continued on to the end of the line.

They found Los Angeles a peaceful little haven that was on the verge of becoming a fashionable winter resort. Still half-somnolent under the spell of its Spanish heritage, it was a civilized California trading post with a kind of pastoral charm. Acres of citrus and avocado groves, vineyards, orchards, and dairy farms stretched westward to the Pacific and eastward to the desert and mountain ranges. It bore none of the *nouveau-riche* cow-town aspect which came later.

Angelenos regarded the burgeoning motion

on several operettas. The first of these was prophetically called *California*.

In 1913, DeMille and Lasky attended a screening of the motion picture *The Great Train Robbery* and were immediately excited about the possibilities of telling a story through the film medium. A few days later, while having lunch at the Claridge Grill in New York, they decided to go into motion picture production and formed the Jesse L. Lasky Feature Play Company. An East Side glove seller, Samuel Goldfish, who later changed his name to Goldwyn, enthusiastically

DeMille smiles down at Bryant Washburn on the set of *Till I Come Back to You* (1918).

picture industry with something akin to the amused tolerance Madrilenos still accord gypsies. Definitely, anybody working in films was not to be accepted socially. Westward, in the peripheral sticks, was a little farming village, nothing more than an unincorporated community, called Hollywood.

Seeking a place to headquarter the Jesse L. Lasky Feature Play Company, DeMille rented a big old barn at what is now the northeastern corner of Vine and Selma. It was no more than a huge stable in which the citrus-grower owner, Jacob Stern, reserved the right to house his horses and carriage. DeMille posted the shingle outside, THE JESSE L. LASKY FEATURE PLAY COMPANY, and here, at 6284 Selma Avenue, in a rented bucolic home, interior shooting began on *The Squaw Man*. Exteriors were photographed

on location in the vast adjacent countryside, which all too soon became valuable real estate. The exteriors selected approximated, and often surpassed, Wyoming terrain.

DeMille told the whole story in his *Autobiography*, edited by Donald Hayne (Prentice-Hall, Inc., 1959), a volume which must be regarded as definitive for any reader wishing to know his full history. But none of those involved in the making of *The Squaw Man* had any inkling of what they were really pioneering. Putting that six-reel feature on film and readying it for release involved as many trials and tribulations as those which afflicted Job, but it placed the Lasky Company soundly on the production program; it was responsible for the formation of Paramount Pictures, Incorporated; and, more importantly, it put Hollywood itself on the map as the film capital of the world, with Cecil B. DeMille the acknowledged father of the Hollywood motion picture industry.

There are not many around now who remember and can appreciate the film career DeMille made for himself. It was a career which, after all, lasted forty-six years, during which time seventy feature films were made that bear his stamp as "Producer-Director." Most filmgoers associate the DeMille name with either the biblical specials he filmed on an epic scale or the exotic bedroom-bathroom social dramas and comedies he made so fashionable. Everybody remembers him as Hollywood's supreme showman, whose most typical and best-liked picture is *The Greatest Show on Earth*, a film which, besides being a box-office bonanza, earned him more critical respect and within-the-industry honors than any other he made.

He himself has noted that it was not until he filmed *Joan the Woman* (1917) that he developed a taste for the spectacular. Generally forgotten are most of the features he directed during the first six years of his career. Those who find it smart to denigrate him prefer to ignore the high regard in which his work as a director was held by critics and film historians during those first years. It has been said that until DeMille discovered the pictorial possibilities of the bathroom and boudoir, no one considered him as an exploiter of sex, nor were such adjectives as "sexy," "cheap," or "vulgar" ever used to describe his films. Among directors, only his name and those of D. W. Griffith and Alfred Hitchcock were really sufficient in themselves to attract top box-office trade.

For audiences today, *Male and Female, Why Change Your Wife?*, or *The Affairs of Anatol* and their luxurious, high-toned goings-on, can, at best, only be viewed as "high camp"; their production, architectural, and costume designs, in particular, are responsible for the term "Early DeMille." If those same audiences, however, were to view the even earlier *The Captive, Kindling, Carmen*, or *The Whispering Chorus*, they would see DeMille in a different light and accord his over-all work a more serious and truer evaluation.

One thing DeMille never forgot: the story he was telling. He was a born storyteller, and his pictures bear ample testimony to that fact. Each successive sequence in *any* DeMille picture advances his story another step. His early training with David Belasco not only gave him a keen understanding of showmanship, but it implanted within him an instinctive sense for narration. He might go from trite to triter or tritest, but the story he had to tell never remained stationary. Through the medium of the camera he became and remained, through silence and sound, an articulate teller of the visual story.

Nor can his pictures really be typed. He produced and directed every kind of story. The first three DeMille films are two westerns and a rugged outdoor adventure story. He filmed many other westerns and outdoor adventure tales, but he also proved himself in comedy, contemporary and period romance, social preachment, domestic drama, historical pageant, fantasy, propaganda, biblical spectacle, musical comedy, suspense, and, the war story. Name the genre, and there is at least one DeMille picture to represent it.

He reigned as King of Paramount for twelve years, and then, when he found front office

DeMille talking over a scene from *The Buccaneer* (1938) with Franciska Gaal.

Theodore Roberts, Jeanie Macpherson,
and DeMille on location for The Ten Commandments (1923).

Pauline Garon and DeMille in
conference with Claire West,
costume designer for *Adam's Rib*
(1923).

Although confined to a cot after he collapsed on the set, DeMille
continued to direct *Union Pacific* (1939). Here he is seen with
Joel McCrea, Barbara Stanwyck, and Richard Lane.

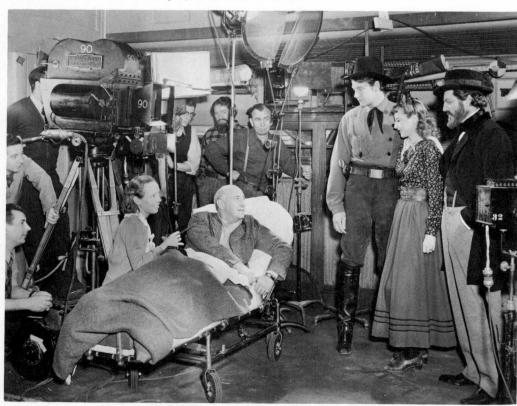

supervision too restricting, went over to Producers Distributing Company, where he had his own unit, personally directing four special features of his own and supervising an entire calendar of program attractions starring players in whose careers he was interested. Subsequently, he produced and directed three of his first talkies at Metro-Goldwyn-Mayer, but in 1932 he trium-

Camera! DeMille (*upper right-hand corner*) directs a scene from *Union Pacific*.

phantly returned to the new Paramount and remained to make the final fifteen pictures of his career. Many of those films are still in distribution, and annually one of the big blockbusters, *Samson and Delilah*, *The Ten Commandments*, or *The Greatest Show on Earth*, is reissued as a deluxe special.

Ironically, when DeMille left Paramount in 1925, D. W. Griffith was engaged by that studio to make the kind of special feature Paramount wanted to exploit. Griffith's Paramount films were hardly among his best, nor, with the single exception of *The King of Kings*, were the pictures DeMille made away from Paramount.

Only D. W. Griffith can be said to have created as many or more screen stars as did DeMille. In his first years, he followed the popular trend established by Famous Players, which was also to release through Paramount, wooing top legitimate actors into film careers. But then he showed a definite preference for taking an unknown or little-known screen player who had only limited camera experience and making him or her a star or featured player of worldwide importance. Gloria Swanson, Bebe Daniels, Wanda Hawley, Agnes Ayres, Leatrice Joy, Nita Naldi, Jacqueline Logan, Vera Reynolds, Jetta Goudal or Wallace Reid, Thomas Meighan, Sessue Hayakawa, Theodore Roberts, Jack Holt, Monte Blue, William Boyd, Rod La Rocque, Joel McCrea, and Robert Preston are only a few who would not have so quickly achieved major importance had their careers not been enhanced at an early period by acting in a DeMille film.

The blizzard sequence, directed by DeMille, from George Melford's *Nan of Music Mountain*, with Wallace Reid, Ann Little, and Theodore Roberts.

DeMille looks over sketches for *North West Mounted Police* (1940).

DeMille and his wife Constance raised a large family: a daughter of their own, Cecelia (now Mrs. Joseph Harper); and two sons and a daughter whom they adopted—John, Richard, and Katherine.

Right up to the end of his life DeMille continued planning or producing new film spectacles. After the 1956 *The Ten Commandments*, many wondered how he could possibly hope to top so gigantic a production. That never bothered him. After its release, when asked, "What are your future plans, Mr. DeMille?", he replied succinctly, "Another picture, or another world." Members of his production crew who had seen him fearlessly ride a giant camera boom to the top of a sound stage or tent, commented drily, "Mr. DeMille will never go to heaven unless he can ride on a boom."

But the sands in the hourglass of his life were running low, and early in the morning of January 21, 1959, he died, aged 77. His death marked the end of an exciting phase of Hollywood film production. The times had already changed, but the DeMille feature never languished for want of an audience. More than any other man, he knew what moviegoers wanted to see, and he gave it to them.

NOTES ON THE FILMS

This book is devoted to the seventy motion pictures which Cecil B. DeMille *personally* directed during his long and enormously successful career (1913 to 1956).

When DeMille accepted the position of Director-General of all productions for the Jesse L. Lasky Feature Play Company, he personally directed those vehicles for which he felt a particular empathy. He also acted as supervisor and consultant on all the feature films produced by the company during its first years. And, occasionally, he directed sequences of certain films assigned and accredited to other directors in order to get them ready to meet release dates. Likewise, he co-authored original screen plays and stories for some of the Lasky films he was too busy to direct himself, and he adapted properties written by others into screen form which were subsequently directed by other men: e.g., *The Love Mask* (1916) had an original DeMille scenario, in collaboration with Jeanie Macpherson, and was directed by Frank Reicher; *The Only Son* (1914) was directed by Oscar C. Apfel from a scenario DeMille had adapted from Winchell Smith's play.

The Squaw Man, the first film he directed, released in February, 1914, is the only picture on which he officially shares credit with another director, Oscar C. Apfel. Actually DeMille did direct parts of other films which Apfel directed, just as Apfel served as what would now be termed a second-unit director for some of the films DeMille directed during those first four busy years (1913 through 1916).

DeMille also wrote scenarios and supervised productions to which he assigned other directors: George Melford, James Neill, Frank Reicher, and Fred Thompson.

Until 1916, when the Lasky Company was absorbed into the giant Paramount parent company, DeMille often assisted these and other Lasky directors on their films. When he took over for George Melford for one day's shooting of the Wallace Reid vehicle, *Nan of Music Mountain*, it happened that the day's shooting involved a blizzard, and with DeMille at the megaphone it became the most colossal blizzard Hollywood had ever experienced. There are publicity photographs extant of studio workers sweeping up the artificial snow which had poured out of the film stage onto the sidewalks and streets of Vine and Selma. That one day's work has also been re-

Showing how Paulette Goddard should be spanked in *North West Mounted Police*.

referred to the work involved in adapting and actually writing the scenarios for filming. Likewise, in that period the term "produced" frequently was used as it is today in the English theater, as meaning "directed."

When DeMille left Famous Players-Lasky in 1925 and joined Producers' Distributing Corporation, he was again active as production supervisor for the program features which starred such players as William Boyd, Jetta Goudal, Rod La Rocque and others he also used in his own specials made at a separate unit.

DeMille acted as supervisor, producer, and narrator for such documentaries as *Land of Liberty* (1940) and *California's Golden Beginning* (1948). Clips from many of his own features were included in the footage. About twenty minutes of the biblical episodes from his 1923 *The Ten Commandments* were included as part of *Forgotten Commandments*, an anti-Communist feature released by Paramount in 1923. The version of *The Sign of the Cross* reissued by Paramount in 1944 was preceded by an eleven-minute prologue, written by Dudley Nichols, involving the crew of an Allied bomber flying over Rome in an argument which stated that American soldiers were then sacrificing their lives for tolerance and freedom in much the same way early Christians accepted martyrdom. A sequence was deleted from DeMille's *The Affairs of Anatol* that was subsequently expanded to a separate feature, *Don't Tell Everything*, directed by Sam Wood.

DeMille directed three productions of *The Squaw Man*: two silent versions (1914 and 1918); and a sound version (1931). He re-made one of his early successes, *The Golden Chance* (1915), as *Forbidden Fruit* (1921). Twenty years after his 1938 version of *The Buccaneer*, he supervised a new production of it that was produced by Henry Wilcoxon and directed by Anthony Quinn (his son-in-law at that time). He utilized the biblical story of Moses twice. It was the first half of his 1923 production of *The Ten Commandments*, but in 1956 he expanded the story of Moses into a full 221-minute special, which is his final film.

At the time of his death in 1959, he had several projects in mind as possible subjects for his seventy-first film. He wanted to make a large-scale, heartwarming picture about the Boy Scout movement; a great deal of research was accumulated for a film about the Old Testament heroine Esther; and he never relinquished the hope of making another religious epic: the life of Mary,

sponsible for the curious error which persistently shows up in film pictorials, where a shot of DeMille directing with Wallace Reid standing beside him at the camera is identified as being from *The Call of the North*. Reid, of course, was never in any version of that film, and the still was actually taken on the set of *Nan of Music Mountain* on the day DeMille directed the blizzard sequence.

An examination of the *Catalog of Copyright Entries* for the films produced by the Lasky Company indicates how many films DeMille was involved in preparing for screening in his capacity as Director-General. He is constantly given a "picturized by" credit, and sometimes he is entitled to such a credit when it is not officially acknowledged. The term "picturized by" is now obsolete, but it was popular at that time and

10

DeMille descends to the ocean floor to direct Ray Milland and John Wayne in an underwater sequence of *Reap the Wild Wind* (1942).

With Mary Pickford and Darryl F. Zanuck at the 1950 Academy Award presentations.

With Anne Baxter on the set of *The Ten Commandments* (1956).

DeMille with Gloria Swanson in *Sunset Boulevard*.

the mother of Jesus Christ, which he wanted to call *The Queen of Queens*. As a story basis he had purchased the rights to a Broadway success, *Family Portrait*, but the Catholic Church was adamantly opposed to depicting the Virgin Mary as being the mother of other children.

Of all the films he directed, his personal favorite was *The King of Kings*. He screened it frequently and always wept unashamedly during its running.

DeMille never relinquished an opportunity to play himself on film, and he made cameo appearances in a score of Paramount films released during the two extended periods he worked at that studio. He also filmed special prologues and

trailers for many of his features, in which he personally addressed his audience before his picture unwound. His appearance as himself in Billy Wilder's *Sunset Boulevard* remains, however, his best performance *before* the cameras.

He also became involved in several plagiarism suits, but, as in the case of the lawsuit over the first version of *The Ten Commandments*, the cases always fell apart when brought to court. The legal charge that the story of *This Day and Age* was a plagiarism of the distinguished German film *M*, was settled out of court, as was the charge that the final sequence of *Feet of Clay* utilized sequences from Sutton Vane's play *Outward Bound*. That sequence had its inspiration in

Mildred Harris

Monte Blue

Geraldine Farrar

Julia Faye

a Beulah Marie Dix play *Beyond the Border*, and Mrs. Dix was co-author of the *Feet of Clay* scenario!

NOTES ON THE STARS AND PLAYERS

DeMille was famous for giving many of the screen's greatest luminaries the roles which catapulted them to top stardom. Gloria Swanson is universally regarded as the DeMille star *par excellence*, and DeMille's appearance with her in *Sunset Boulevard* confirmed that opinion in the public mind.

Like other noted directors, DeMille surrounded himself with a loyal and dependable staff and crew and he formed a permanent group of players whom he consistently employed in what became his personal stock company. A born executive, he knew the value of delegating work to people he could trust. He was very loyal to actors working for him; he might be a martinet, but if he respected their talents, he used them time and again. For instance, one of Mildred Harris' early appearances on the screen was a small ingénue role in his 1915 *The Warrens of Virginia*; six years later, in 1921, she was his sirenish lead in *Fool's Paradise*; in 1942 she was among the bit players in *Reap the Wild Wind*; and, in 1944, towards the end of her life, he gave her another bit in *The Story of Dr. Wassell*. Much the same is true of Monte Blue, who first appeared for DeMille in the 1918 version of *The Squaw Man*, rose to starring roles in *Something to Think About* (1920) and *The Affairs of Anatol* (1921), and was playing bits in *Union Pacific* (1939), *North West Mounted Police* (1940), and *Reap the Wild Wind* (1942).

Geraldine Farrar and Gloria Swanson tie as actresses playing more leads for DeMille than any of his other female stars. Each starred in six DeMille pictures. Julia Faye, however, played in more DeMille films than any other actress. She appeared in every kind of role, from maids to second leads, in thirty-one DeMille features, starting with *The Woman God Forgot* (1917) to the 1956 *The Ten Commandments*.

Elliott Dexter played more leads for DeMille than any other masculine star, eleven. His nearest competitor is Wallace Reid, who starred in seven DeMille pictures. Theodore Roberts and Raymond Hatton, however, tie as actors who appeared in more DeMille features than any other male players. Each of them played twenty-three roles for him.

14

Perhaps it should be pointed out that in at least two cases players who bear the same names as noted contemporary actors are not the same men. James Mason and William Holden, character actors in DeMille films, are not the stars known today by those names.

The spelling of proper names in early motion picture days was maddeningly inconsistent. An attempt has been made here to make consistent the spelling of names to conform with that which the player in question eventually settled on as preferred.

Theodore Roberts

Gloria Swanson

Wallace Reid

16

Elliott Dexter

Raymond Hatton

PART 1

THE
SILENT FILMS

Cowboy cast

Joseph E. Singleton and Red Wing

THE SQUAW MAN

Produced and directed by Cecil B. DeMille and Oscar C. Apfel. Scenario by DeMille and Apfel, adapted by Edwin Milton Royle from his play. Cameraman: Alfred Gandolfi. Film Editor: Mamie Wagner. Released by Jesse L. Lasky Feature Play Co., February 15, 1914. Six reels.

STORY

Captain James Wynnegate and his cousin Henry, Earl of Kerhill, are joint custodians of charity funds. Wynnegate suddenly leaves England, tacitly accepting blame for the embezzlement of the funds because he loves his cousin's wife, Lady Diana, and knows her husband to be the guilty one. Wynnegate goes out west to Wyoming, where he makes an enemy of Cash Hawkins, cattle rustler, most powerful villain in the West. Wynnegate rescues an Indian girl, Nat-U-Rich, from Cash's advances, and she subsequently saves Wynnegate from death and nurses him back to health. He marries Nat-U-Rich when he learns she is to bear a child, and she kills Wynnegate's enemy, Cash Hawkins. Lady Diana arrives in Wyoming to inform Wynnegate that her husband has been killed while big game hunting, but before dying has confessed to the embezzlement, and that Wynnegate is now the Earl of Kerhill. Nat-U-Rich commits suicide when the Sheriff discovers she is the killer of Cash Hawkins, and Wynnegate, with his half-breed son and Lady Diana, returns to England as the new Earl of Kerhill.

21

Cast of *The Squaw Man*

Baby DeRue and Dick LeStrange

CAST

Captain James Wynnegate	Dustin Farnum
Henry, Earl of Kerhill	Monroe Salisbury
Diana, Countess of Kerhill	Winifred Kingston
Nat-U-Rich	Red Wing
Cash Hawkins	Billy Elmer
Grouchy	Dick La Strange
Sir John	Foster Knox
Tabywana	Joe E. Singleton
Big Bill	Dick La Reno
Mr. Petrie	Fred Montague
Hal	Baby de Rue
The Dowager Lady Kerhill	Mrs. A. W. Filson
Lady Mabel Wynnegate	Haidee Fuller

22

Billy Elmer, Red Wing,
Dustin Farnum,
Dick LaReno,
and Joseph E. Singleton

Baby DeRue, Winifred Kingston,
Joseph E. Singleton, Dustin Farnum,
and Red Wing

Winifred Kingston, Dustin Farnum, and cowboys

REVIEWS

"Without risking dangerous comparisons, it is only fair to place *The Squaw Man* among the few really satisfactory film adaptations of plays. In point of sustained interest it gives place to none; the acting offers no cause for criticism, the settings are notably appropriate, and, best of all, there is a real story told in photographed action, not in lengthy subtitles, illustrated by fragmentary scenes."

The New York Dramatic Mirror,
February 25, 1914.

"It is quite probable that both Royle and DeMille, when they come to study this characterization from the viewpoint of spectators, will realize that the art of producing moving pictures is to be measured by its own canons alone. Both may perceive that this new method of thought transmission has a grander scope than the boxed-in stage presentation once they are enfolded in the charm of its method of telling a story. Its directness, the lack of intervening utterance, its very silence, all contribute to a fascination long proven to exist, not only for the mixed audience, but for those familiar with superior examples of the older arts. When these gentlemen come to us, as they surely will, with the finest products of their creative talent, unhampered by what they have learned in a totally different medium of expression, with a cause that is compelling, it will be with quickened fondness for what can give such free release to their forces."

Louis Reeves Harrison in
The Moving Picture World,
February 28, 1914.

"Of course we talked things over and built the story for the picture—which, by the way, was remarkably easy. You may rest assured, however, I will make it a condition in my next contract that I am to have the privilege of being around when the work of direction is going on. Yes, I realize that the technique of the screen is one thing, while the technique of the stage is quite another thing. At the same time, I believe that the man with a considerable stage experience may be permitted to offer suggestions. Some of them may be impracticable, others may be valuable...."

Excerpt from an interview
with Edwin Milton Royle,
written by W. Stephen Bush, in
The Moving Picture World,
February 21, 1914.

Red Wing, Dustin Farnum, and cowboys

Joseph E. Singleton, Dustin Farnum,
Red Wing, and Billy Elmer

Winifred Kingston, Monroe Salisbury,
Foster Knox, Billy Elmer, and Dustin Farnum

Dustin Farnum and Red Wing

Dustin Farnum and Billy Elmer

Robert Edeson and players

Horace B. Carpenter,
Theodore Roberts, and
Winifred Kingston

THE CALL OF THE NORTH

Produced and directed by Cecil B. DeMille. Scenario by DeMille, based on Stewart Edward White's novel, Conjuror's House, *and the play dramatized therefrom by George Broadhurst. Cameraman: Alvin Wyckoff. Film Editor: Mamie Wagner. Released by Jesse L. Lasky Feature Play Co., August 15, 1914. Five reels.*

STORY

Ned Stewart, a free trader, learns from an aged priest how his father, Graehme Stewart, had been unjustly accused of adultery with the trading post factor's wife, and killed. Ned hunts down the villain responsible for wronging his father, but is caught and sent on *la longue traverse* (the long journey to death). He is saved by the heroine, Virginia, who loves him, and his father's name is cleared when the villain, on his deathbed seeking absolution, confesses his perfidies. Ned and Virginia find happiness together.

DeMille and entire cast

CAST

Graehme Stewart	⎱ Robert Edeson
Ned Stewart	⎰
Galen Albert	Theodore Roberts
Virginia	Winifred Kingston
Rand	Horace B. Carpenter
Elodie	Florence Dagmar
Me-en-gan	Milton Brown
Julie	Vera McGarry
Picard	Jode Mullaly
McTavish	Sydney Deane
Jack Wilson	Fred Montague

"The Call of the North is the latest and beyond question the best of the Lasky photoplays produced under the direction of Cecil B. DeMille and Oscar C. Apfel. In fact, one may glance through the full list of American-made pictures and find no names that stand for higher accomplishment, and few—very few—that signify anything half so satisfying in the nature of a film interpretation of a novel."

The New York Dramatic Mirror,
August 19, 1914.

"Such pictures as these amply confirm my faith in the approaching kingdom of quality. The dominant characteristic of the play is lavishness. A lofty ambition to attain the highest ideals in the motion picture art gave birth to this feature, which I am tempted to describe as one of the greatest classics ever produced on American soil. The theme is classic, its treatment is classic, the atmosphere is classic. Best of all, the theme is distinctly of the New World; it deals with one of the strangest and most romantic phases of life in the Far North."

W. Stephen Bush in
The Moving Picture World,
August 22, 1914.

Robert Edeson, Winifred Kingston, and
Theodore Roberts

Dustin Farnum

Winifred Kingston,
Monroe Salisbury,
Anita King,
and Dustin Farnum

Winifred Kingston and Dustin Farnum

THE VIRGINIAN

Produced and directed by Cecil B. DeMille. Scenario also by DeMille, adapted from the novel by Owen Wister. Cameraman: Alvin Wyckoff. Film Editors: Mamie Wagner and DeMille. Produced by Jesse L. Lasky Feature Play Co., for release by the Paramount Pictures Corp., September 7, 1914. Five reels.

STORY

Pretty Molly Wood becomes the schoolteacher at Bess Creek, Wyoming, where she meets and is attracted by a happy-go-lucky cowboy known as "the Virginian." He is compelled to assist in the hanging of Steve, his best friend, when Steve goes wrong and becomes involved with a band of cattle thieves. Trampas, villainous leader of the thieves, tangles with the Virginian, and boldly calls him a vulgar name. He is grimly advised, "When you call me that—smile." Eventually, the entire band of thieves is run to the ground, and Trampas, in a showdown, is killed by the Virginian, who then wins the hand of the pretty schoolteacher.

Dustin Farnum,
J. W. Johnstone,
and Horace B. Carpenter

CAST

The Virginian	Dustin Farnum
Steve	J. W. Johnston
Uncle Hughey	Sydney Deane
Mr. Ogden	Monroe Salisbury
Mrs. Ogden	Anita King
Trampas	Billy Elmer
Molly Wood	Winifred Kingston
Lin McLean	Hosea Steelman
Stage Driver	James Griswold
Spanish Ed	Horace B. Carpenter
Shorty	Tex Driscoll
Balaam	Dick La Reno
Mrs. Balaam	Mrs. Lewis McCord

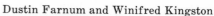

Dustin Farnum and Winifred Kingston

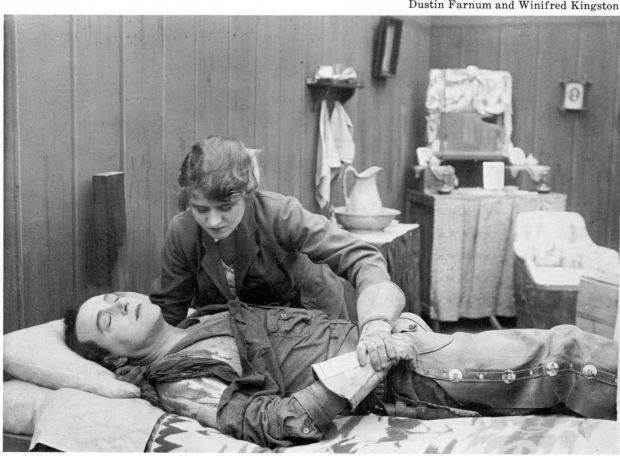

32

DeMille and Dustin Farnum

Dustin Farnum and Winifred Kingston

Dustin Farnum and Winifred Kingston

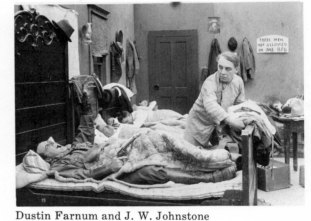

Dustin Farnum and J. W. Johnstone

Dustin Farnum and Winifred Kingston

REVIEWS

"Drama, comedy and photographic spectacle are the triple alliance met in the picturization of Owen Wister's story. They win out very easily. The strength of the dramatic and spectacular elements were to be expected; but comedy is a less familiar attribute of virile tales of the West. Needless to say, it adds immensely to the entertainment value of a film, even when the director is dealing with a more or less serious subject."

The New York Dramatic Mirror,
September 9, 1914.

"To realize the singular advantages of the film over the stage in first-class productions, particularly in those where an exterior atmosphere prevails throughout, one but has to view the Jesse Lasky multiple reel of Owen Wister's play of the plains. To those who have seen the play, and they are probably in the majority, the possibilities of this production are very plain, for most of the action occurs in the open. The story of the original book is followed throughout with the gun duel between Trampas and the Virginian utilized further on with a pretty picture."

The Weekly *Variety*,
September 11, 1914.

"Most engaging of matinee idols, even in filmland, is Dustin Farnum, as *The Virginian*, at Tally's, this week. He is entirely irresistible as the big, handsome, boyish frontiersman, who deals out even-handed justice, plays tricks on everybody, and at last makes the schoolma'am love him. Some splendid horsemanship is shown, and the rugged mountain scenery amid which the action of the story is laid adds greatly to the charm of the picture."

Grace Kingsley in
The Los Angeles Daily Times,
September 15, 1914.

Dustin Farnum and players.

Max Figman and Cecelia DeMille

36

WHAT'S HIS NAME

Produced and directed by Cecil B. DeMille. Scenario also by DeMille, adapted from the novel by George Barr McCutcheon. Cameraman: Alvin Wyckoff. Film Editor: Cecil B. DeMille. Produced by Jesse L. Lasky Feature Play Co., for release by the Paramount Pictures Corp., October 22, 1914. Five reels.

STORY

In Blakeville, N.Y., there is no more popular young man than Harvey, who runs the town's soda fountain. He marries Nellie, the baker's daughter, and for three years they are happy, although poor. Then a musical comedy company comes to town, and Nellie is discovered as an actress. Harvey travels with his wife on tour, eventually losing his own identity and becoming only "What's-His-Name." When Nellie becomes infatuated with a millionaire, Harvey takes their small daughter and returns to Blakeville, while Nellie goes to Reno for a divorce. The child's subsequent serious illness brings Harvey and Nellie together again.

CAST

Harvey	Max Figman
Nellie	Lolita Robertson
Uncle Peter	Sydney Deane
Best Man	Dick La Strange
Friend of Nellie's	Merta Carpenter
Fairfax	Fred Montague
Character Man	Theodore Roberts
Phoebe, the child	Cecelia DeMille

REVIEWS

"Here is one of those stories without any pretense that has things in it as deep as the human soul . . . . The production must have been difficult on account of the condensation, but it is filled with signs of good direction."

Hanford C. Judson in
The Moving Picture World,
November 7, 1914.

"The scenes in a theatre, of which there are many, are presented with much convincing detail to show the bloomer-clad chorus girls being drilled into unity of action, and later the spectacular results achieved by the finished article, set off against the glittering stage devices indispensable to musical comedy. A Los Angeles theatre was used in obtaining realistic effects that would have been difficult to duplicate in a motion picture studio."

The New York Dramatic Mirror,
October 28, 1914.

Max Figman and Lolita Robertson

DeMille directing Max Figman and
Lolita Robertson

Anita King,
Horace B. Carpenter,
and Mabel Van Buren

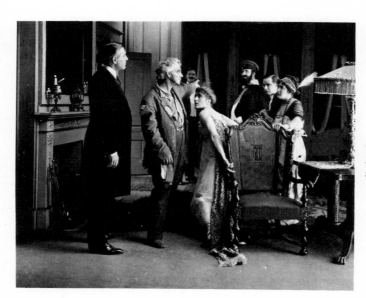

Charles Richman,
Anita King,
and Theodore Roberts

40

Charles Richman, Fred Montague,
and Theodore Roberts

THE MAN FROM HOME

Produced and directed by Cecil B. DeMille. Scenario also by DeMille, adapted from the play by Booth Tarkington and Harry Leon Wilson. Cameraman: Alvin Wyckoff. Film Editor: Cecil B. DeMille. Produced by the Jesse L. Lasky Feature Play Co. for release by the Paramount Pictures Corp., November 9, 1914. Five reels.

STORY

Daniel Pike is appointed executor of a fortune inherited by the Simpson son and daughter, Horace and Ethel, who go to Europe, where, as vulnerable Americans, they meet and are attracted by a group of traveling Russian fortune-hunters. Pike arrives and tries to prevent the marriage of Ethel to a foppish member of the fortune-hunting group. Aided by the Grand Duke Vasill, who exposes the group as money-hungry opportunists, Pike is successful.

41

CAST

Daniel Voorhees Pike	Charles Richman
The Grand Duke Vasill	Theodore Roberts
Earl of Hawcastle	Fred Montague
Hon. Almerc St. Aubyn	Monroe Salisbury
Ivanoff	Horace B. Carpenter
Horace Granger Simpson	Jode Mullaly
Old Man Simpson	Dick La Reno
Ethel Granger Simpson	Mabel Van Buren
Helene, Countess	
De Champigney	Anita King
Officer of Gendarmes	James Neill
Ribiere	Robert Fleming
Prefect of Italian Police	J. W. Johnston
Ivanoff's Maid	Florence Dagmar

Charles Richman, Theodore Roberts,
Mabel Van Buren, and Jode Mullaly

Mabel Van Buren

Monroe Salisbury,
Theodore Roberts,
and Mabel Van Buren

Horace B. Carpenter, Anita King,
and Fred Montague

REVIEWS

"The Lasky Company will be obliged to aim at and attain an exceptionally high goal if it intends to surpass the almost unequalled merit of *The Man from Home* in the future. It has not been our pleasure to view all of this company's productions, but of all that we have seen this is by all odds the best."

Peter Milne in
The Motion Picture News,
November 21, 1914.

"Cecil B. DeMille has injected quite a bit of drama into the quietly humorous play, originally acted with William Hodge in the role of Daniel Voorhees Pike. Lasky's director-general brings the story to approximately the same conclusion, but he travels a very different path in doing so,

and the scenes that loom large along the way belong exclusively to the picture."

The New York Dramatic Mirror,
November 18, 1914.

"Here is a shining star in the Paramount sky. *The Man from Home* is a good deal more than a successful film feature. It is a veritable triumph of screen dramatization. It emphasizes in a thoroughly convincing manner that, as a medium of dramatic expression, the film has no metes and bounds. A play in which so much seemed to depend on the dialogue has been adapted for the screen absolutely without loss of any values either of dramatic action or of characterization."

W. Stephen Bush in
The Moving Picture World,
November 21, 1914.

Mabel Van Buren and Charles Richman

Bessie Barriscale and Monroe Salisbury

J. W. Johnstone
and Bessie Barriscale

46

Bessie Barriscale and J. W. Johnstone

ROSE OF THE RANCHO

Produced and directed by Cecil B. DeMille. Scenario also by DeMille, adapted from the play by David Belasco and Richard Walton Tully. Cameraman: Alvin Wyckoff. Film Editor: Cecil B. DeMille. Produced by the Jesse L. Lasky Feature Play Co. for release by the Paramount Pictures Corp., November 15, 1914. Five reels.

STORY

When Esra Kincaid and his band of outlaws take the Espinoza ranch by force, killing the owner and forcing his daughter to take her own life, the U.S., represented by a government agent named Kearney, takes over. He falls in love with the beautiful Juanita, daughter of the Castro rancho, and then learns that Kincaid has the Castros marked as his next victims. Kearney intervenes, holding off the outlaws until the cavalry arrives, whereafter he is able to declare his love for Juanita, "Rose of the Rancho."

J. W. Johnstone and Bessie Barriscale

Bessie Barriscale and cast in siege sequence

Jane Darwell, Bessie Barriscale,
and J. W. Johnstone

49

REVIEWS

"David Belasco voiced the feelings of probably everyone of the audience when, so it is reported, he said, 'This is better than the play.'"

William A. Johnston in
The Motion Picture News,
November 28, 1914.

"To use a colloquial phrase, *Rose of the Rancho* has everything. The story as prepared for pictures makes interesting romantic drama; the settings representing California in the middle of the last century are superb, the essential characters are notably well presented by one of the strongest casts yet gathered for a Lasky picture, and the photography and tinting are flawless."

The New York Dramatic Mirror,
November 25, 1914.

Dick LaReno and
Jeanie Macpherson

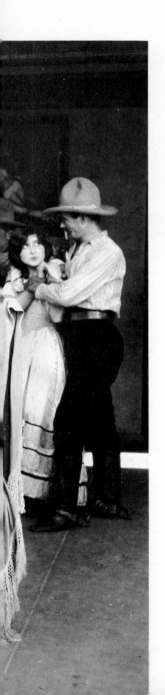

Bessie Barriscale

House Peters and Mabel Van Buren

Tex Driscoll,
Theodore Roberts, and Jeanie Macpherson

THE GIRL OF THE GOLDEN WEST

Produced and directed by Cecil B. DeMille. Scenario also by DeMille, based on the play by David Belasco. Cameraman: Alvin Wyckoff. Film Editor: Cecil B. DeMille. Produced by the Jesse L. Lasky Feature Play Co. for release by the Paramount Pictures Corp., January 4, 1915. Five reels.

STORY

Ramerrez, a road agent, is loved by the Girl, who does not know his background. He is forced to take refuge in the Girl's store and saloon, and she hides him from the Sheriff, who, knowing that Ramerrez has to be hiding there, agrees to settle the man's fate in a card game with the Girl. She wins her lover's safety—and when Ramerrez is followed by the Sheriff and nearly hanged, the Girl saves him again, and they are allowed to ride off together.

Theodore Roberts and Mabel Van Buren

CAST

The Girl	Mabel Van Buren
Rance	Theodore Roberts
Ramerrez	House Peters
Wowkle	Anita King
Sidney Duck	Sydney Deane
Ashby	Billy Elmer
Nina	Jeanie Macpherson
Castro	Raymond Hatton
Senor Slim	Dick La Strange
Nick, the Bartender	Tex Driscoll
Antonio	Art Ortego
Stage Coach Driver	John Ortego
Guard	James Griswold
Old Minstrel	Ed. Harley

House Peters, Theodore Roberts, and Mabel Van Buren

House Peters and Mabel Van Buren

54

REVIEWS

"First a drama, then an opera, and now a triumph for the world of film is the story of Lasky's *The Girl of the Golden West*. Great pains seem to have been taken to secure the proper location for the exteriors, and the mountain views are marvels of clear, perfect photography. In fact, it is only fair to the producers to state that the entire five reels, from the opening sequence to the beautiful sunrise effect at the finale, are wonderful examples of what can be done by competent cameramen and directors."

H. S. Fuld in
The Motion Picture News,
January 16, 1915.

"Cecil B. DeMille never made a truer adaptation of a play, following the story in its essentials and amplifying, as only pictures can amplify, the action that in a stage production must be omitted. He has been liberal in his use of glorious California locations and free in the development of the story, looking at it from the viewpoint of a maker of photoplays determined to utilize the best possibilities of his medium. He treated the subject from a new angle, and audiences, no matter how many times they have seen the drama on the stage, will find in the film version novelty and dramatic force. *The Girl of the Golden West* is as fresh as though it were written yesterday."

The New York Dramatic Mirror,
January 13, 1915.

House Peters and Mabel Van Buren

Theodore Roberts,
House Peters, and Mabel Van Buren

House Peters and Mabel Van Buren

House Peters
and Mabel Van Buren

56

Theodore Roberts and Mabel Van Buren

Theodore Roberts, Mabel Van Buren,
and House Peters

Battle scene

Blanche Sweet and House Peters

House Peters and Blanche Sweet

THE WARRENS OF VIRGINIA

Produced and directed by Cecil B. DeMille. Scenario by William C. de Mille, based upon his own play. Presented by Jesse L. Lasky in association with David Belasco. Cameraman: Alvin Wyckoff. Film Editor: Cecil B. DeMille. Produced by the Jesse L. Lasky Feature Play Co. for release by the Paramount Pictures Corp., February 15, 1915. Five reels.

STORY

At the beginning of America's Civil War, Ned Burton parts from his Southern sweetheart, Agatha Warren, and joins the Union forces. When Burton, as a special correspondent, tries to learn about a supply train's arrival, he is sheltered by Agatha, who still loves him, although she is torn by her loyalty to the Confederacy. Burton is saved from death by the war's end, and Agatha and he make up their differences and marry.

CAST

Agatha Warren	Blanche Sweet
General Warren	James Neill
Arthur Warren	Page Peters
Mrs. Warren	Mabel Van Buren
Betty Warren	Marguerite House
Ned Burton	House Peters
General Griffin	Dick La Reno
Sapho, the colored servant	Mrs. Lewis McCord

(Mildred Harris is credited as playing
a small role, as is also Marjorie Daw.)

House Peters and Blanche Sweet

Mabel Van Buren,
Marjorie Daw,
and Blanche Sweet

REVIEWS

"By far the best feature of the picture . . . were the martial incidents, the ragged, starving Confederate troops, their better conditioned enemies, the battle behind the trenches and the ambushing and destruction of the supply train."

The New York Dramatic Mirror,
February 14, 1915.

"Contrasting conditions of the South before, and near the close of the Civil War, camp life of the two armies the day before the ending of hostilities, and realistic battle scenes, impossible in the stage production of the successful Belasco production, *The Warrens of Virginia,* are featured in the film version in such a true to life manner that this subject is worthy of being termed educational."

J. C. Jessen,
The Motion Picture News,
February 20, 1915.

House Peters and Blanche Sweet

Dick LaReno,
House Peters, Page Peters,
Blanche Sweet, James Neill,
and Mabel Van Buren

House Peters

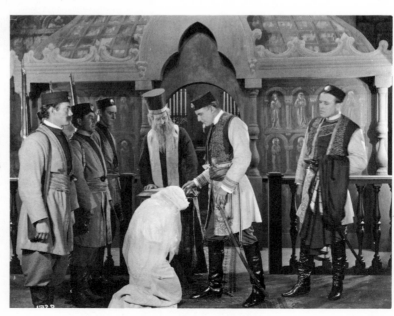

Rita Jolivet,
House Peters,
and Page Peters

62

Lawrence Peyton and Rita Jolivet

THE UNAFRAID

Produced and directed by Cecil B. DeMille. Scenario also by DeMille, adapted from the novel by Eleanor M. Ingram. Cameraman: Alvin Wyckoff. Film Editor: Cecil B. DeMille. Produced by the Jesse L. Lasky Feature Play Co. for release by the Paramount Pictures Corp., April 1, 1915. Four reels.

STORY

Two Montenegrin brothers plot to kidnap an American heiress, Delight Warren. The older brother, Stefan, waylays her while she is traveling through a mountain pass, and, abducting her, forces her to marry him so that he will have a hold on her wealth. Then the two fall in love, and Stefan is compelled to protect her from the villainies of his younger brother, Michael. When Michael is killed, Stefan offers to return her to America, where she can obtain a divorce—but the girl prefers to stay in Montenegro as her husband's wife.

House Peters, Marjorie Daw,
and Rita Jolivet

Delight Warren	Rita Jolivet
Stefan Balsic	House Peters
Michael Balsic	Page Peters
Jack McCarty	Billy Elmer
Danilo Lesendra	Lawrence Peyton
Secret Agent of Dual Empire	Theodore Roberts
Joseph	Al Ernest Garcia
Irenya	Marjorie Daw
Russian Valet	Raymond Hatton
Countess Novna	Gertrude Kellar

REVIEWS

"The Unafraid" makes a very pleasant and exciting romantic picture. The Montenegrin atmosphere is well carried out. The natural air

House Peters,
Rita Jolivet,
and Page Peters

of distinction of Miss Jolivet and also of House Peters add to the general effect. And don't forget that little Marjorie Daw, whoever she may be, is a real discovery and a comer."

George D. Proctor in
The Motion Picture News,
April 10, 1915.

"In picturizing a play or adapting a novel, Lasky is almost certain of logic, sequence, and—wherein lies the real art—drama. For it has Cecil DeMille, who is more than a director. He is a film architect who used, in this case, the rough plans outlined in the romantic novel of the same name. That he builded so well is quite a film feather in his cap, for some of his materials were of the kind to try the mettle of the best picture constructor."

The New York Dramatic Mirror,
April 7, 1915.

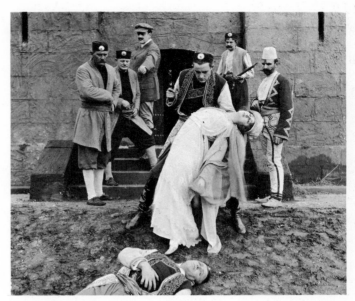

Page Peters, Rita Jolivet,
and House Peters (*on ground*)

House Peters (*center*)

65

Blanche Sweet

Blanche Sweet and House Peters

Blanche Sweet and House Peters

Blanche Sweet and Page Peters

66

Blanche Sweet, House Peters,
and Marjorie Daw

THE CAPTIVE

*Produced and directed by Cecil B. DeMille.
Scenario by DeMille and Jeanie Macpherson,
adapted from their own story. Cameraman:
Alvin Wyckoff. Film Editor: Cecil B. DeMille.
Produced by the Jesse L. Lasky Feature Play Co.
for release by the Paramount Pictures Corp.,
April 22, 1915. Five reels.*

STORY

Because her young brother is killed, Sonya is given a Turkish captive to do her hard work on the farm. Spiteful and revengeful at first, she soon admits to herself that the captive means something more than a common worker to her. The Turks retake the village, and the captive, Mahmud, saves Sonya from harm by striking a superior officer. When peace is declared, he finds that because of that blow, he has forfeited the rights to his noble lands. Similarly, Sonya is dispossessed, her house burned. She takes to the road, and meets up with Mahmud. Having lost all, they both find they have gained everything in their mutual love.

Blanche Sweet and Gerald Ward

Blanche Sweet and House Peters

CAST

Sonya, Montenegrin peasant	Blanche Sweet
Mahmud	House Peters
Marko	Page Peters
Turkish Officer	Theodore Roberts
Milos	Gerald Ward

(Jeanie Macpherson, Marjorie Daw,
and Billy Elmer also in cast.)

REVIEWS

"Blanche Sweet's second experience with the Lasky Company . . . is in every way satisfying, for in *The Captive,* a five-part picturization of a play by Cecil B. DeMille and Jeanie Macpherson,

Blanche Sweet and House Peters

she has a role of possibilities well in keeping with her personality and histrionic method."

Robert C. McElvray in
The Moving Picture World,
May 1, 1915.

"Few external influences go to mar a gradually growing love story that is, so to speak, played across the boards for all it is worth. We are granted three almost uninterrupted reels of Blanche Sweet and House Peters in a plausibly romantic and somewhat strange situation and on this alone the offering must win or fail. There would seem to be, however, small possibility of this latter eventuality, for the two principal parts are in good hands."

The New York Dramatic Mirror,
April 28, 1915.

Gerald Ward, Blanche Sweet,
and House Peters

House Peters and Blanche Sweet

Tom Forman and Ina Claire

Ina Claire and Tom Forman

THE WILD GOOSE CHASE

Produced and directed by Cecil B. DeMille. Scenario by William C. de Mille, adapted from his own play. Cameraman: Alvin Wyckoff. Film editor: Cecil B. DeMille. Produced by the Jesse L. Lasky Feature Play Co. for release by the Paramount Pictures Corp., May 27, 1915. Four reels.

STORY

Two American grandfathers in France decide to give their respective granddaughter and grandson fortunes if they wed. The grandchildren, however, perversely will not accept a marriage arranged for them, and both run away from their respective homes. Both also become members of the same theatrical troup, where they fall in love—and eventually learn that this is exactly what their grandparents had intended them to do.

71

CAST

Betty Wright	Ina Claire
Her Mother	Helen Marlborough
Her Henpecked Father	Raymond Hatton
Bob Randall	Tom Forman
His Father	Ernest Joy
His Mother	Florence Smith
The "Grind"	Lucien Littlefield
Horatio Brutus Bangs	Theodore Roberts

REVIEWS

"For a refined and really funny comedy, enacted by an enthusiastic cast and produced

Ina Claire, Tom Forman, and Theodore Roberts

Ina Claire

72

exceedingly well, *The Wild Goose Chase* has no superiors that we have seen."

Peter Milne in
The Motion Picture News,
June 12, 1915.

"Ina Claire's debut in pictures adds one of the musical comedy stars of magnitude to those who have succumbed to the lure of the studio. The same personality that helped to put over her songs, that endeared her as *The Quaker Girl*, succeeds in making a distinct part of her character here. She is vivacious, demure, pretty, and also likable."

The New York Dramatic Mirror,
June 2, 1915.

73

Edgar Selwyn,
Horace B. Carpenter, and Gertrude Robinson

Edgar Selwyn

Gertrude Robinson and Edgar Selwyn

THE ARAB

Produced and directed by Cecil B. DeMille. Scenario by Edgar Selwyn and Cecil B. DeMille, adapted from the play by Edgar Selwyn. Cameraman: Alvin Wyckoff. Film Editor: Cecil B. DeMille. Produced by the Jesse L. Lasky Feature Play Co. for release by the Paramount Pictures Corp., June 14, 1915. Four reels.

STORY

To chastise his son Jamil for robbing a desert caravan, the old Sheik gives the young man's favorite horse to the offended merchant, who sells it to a Turkish general, who, in turn, bestows it upon a young Christian mission teacher, Mary Hilbert. When Jamil finds that the girl is the new owner of his horse, he takes it away from her, forcing her to walk home through the desert sands. But then he falls in love with Mary and saves her and her father's lives when the Christians are massacred. The old Sheik dies, and Jamil bids Mary farewell, relinquishing love to become the new sheik.

Horace B. Carpenter,
Gertrude Robinson, and Edgar Selwyn

Jamil, the son	Edgar Selwyn
The Sheik, his father	Horace B. Carpenter
Abdullah, the latter's aide	Milton Brown
Meshur, his enemy	Billy Elmer
Dr. Hilbert, of the mission	Sydney Deane
Mary, his daughter	Gertrude Robinson
Ibrahim, servant	J. Parke Jones
Turkish Governor	Theodore Roberts
Mysterious Messenger	Raymond Hatton
American Tourist	Irvin S. Cobb

REVIEWS

"Edgar Selwyn, author and producer of *The Arab* as a play, here stars in a screen visualization of the same subject. It is an exceedingly original offering from first to last, and as pro-

A74

duced the picture lifts the spectator from his seat and for the time being transports him to Arabia, so realistic is the atmosphere."

Peter Milne in
The Motion Picture News,
June 26, 1915.

"After seeing the Lasky version of *The Arab,* you will probably feel that there is not much more to see about this play, and personally, if the screen version were shown on one side of the street and the dialogue play across the way, we should prefer to spend the time at the photoplay, because the screen represents the drama plus so much in the way of outdoor beauty, real desert stuff, and Arabian motion and impetus and intrigue that there can be no comparison between the two."

The New York Dramatic Mirror,
June 23, 1915.

Irvin S. Cobb and Edgar Selwyn

Ernest Joy, Victor Moore, and Anita King

Victor Moore,
Anita King, and Camille Astor

Victor Moore

CHIMMIE FADDEN

Produced and directed by Cecil B. DeMille. Scenario also by DeMille, adapted from the book and play by E. W. Townsend. Cameraman: Alvin Wyckoff. Film Editor: Cecil B. DeMille. Produced by the Jesse L. Lasky Feature Play Co. for release by the Paramount Pictures Corp., June 28, 1915. Four reels.

STORY

Chimmie Fadden, a young Bowery tough, meets a lady doing social work at the settlement house, and is bowled over by her kindness. She saves him from a false arrest, and then installs him, his crooked brother, and his mother in her home as servants. Chimmie foils his brother's plans to make off with the lady's silver, and at the end of the picture finally gets up enough nerve to kiss the French maid.

CAST

Chimmie Fadden	Victor Moore
Larry, his brother	Raymond Hatton
Mrs. Fadden, their mother	Mrs. Lewis McCord
Van Cortlandt, a millionaire	Ernest Joy
Fanny, his daughter	Anita King
Hortense, the French maid	Camille Astor
Antoine, the butler-thief	Tom Forman
Perkins, the butler	Harry DeRoy

Camille Astor
and Victor Moore

REVIEWS

" 'Chimmie Fadden,' the clever creation of Mr. Townsend when he was on the staff of *The New York Sun*, has found a most apt and amusing interpreter in Victor Moore.... It is due to the director to mention the fact that he caught all the happy spirit and all the descriptive power of the author. The atmosphere is splendid, both on the lower East Side with its struggling human beehive and its picturesqueness, and of the Fifth Avenue section. The contrast is consequently all the more effective. Of the settings and the photography and the types I can say no more than that they are up to the best Lasky standard, which is indeed saying a good deal."

W. Stephen Bush in
The Moving Picture World,
July 10, 1915.

"*Chimmie Fadden* is a delightful picture. The major portion of it is devoted to the expression of spontaneous comedy. A minor section of it is employed to introduce dramatic moments that cap the humorous story with an effective climax which could not be conveyed by farcical action. And besides the serious scenes furnish relief to one's aching sides."

Peter Milne in
The Motion Picture News,
July 10, 1915.

Victor Moore, Raymond Hatton, and Tom Forman

Slum street scene

Charlotte Walker,
Thomas Meighan, and Raymond Hatton

82

Charlotte Walker and Thomas Meighan

KINDLING

Produced and directed by Cecil B. DeMille. Scenario also by DeMille, adapted from the play by Charles A. Kenyon. Cameraman: Alvin Wyckoff. Film Editor: Cecil B. DeMille. Produced by the Lasky Feature Play Co. for release by the Paramount Pictures Corp., July 12, 1915. Four reels.

STORY

Maggie Schultz, a young tenement wife about to become a mother, unwittingly becomes the pawn of a gang of crooks who use her in their burglaries. Caught, Maggie protests, "I lied—I fought—I stole to keep my baby from being born in this rathole—and now he's going to be born in jail." But the tenement owner refuses to prosecute, and a happier future is foreseen for the Schultzes.

Florence Dagmar,
Billy Elmer,
Thomas Meighan,
and Charlotte Walker

84

CAST

Maggie Schultz	Charlotte Walker
"Honest" Heine Schultz	Thomas Meighan
Steve, a crook	Raymond Hatton
Mrs. Bates, his mother	Mrs. Lewis McCord
Rafferty, of the Central Office	Billy Elmer
Mrs. Burke-Smith	Lillian Langdon
Alice, her niece	Florence Dagmar
Young Dr. Taylor	Tom Forman

REVIEWS

"I do not hesitate to say that this is one of the best samples of the Lasky school of motion picture art. When at its best this new school beggars comparison. It is pleasing, it is powerful, it scores in every scene, and there are no weak links."

W. Stephen Bush in
The Moving Picture World,
July 24, 1915.

"*Kindling* makes a screen feature of exceptional worth, just as it made a strong play. One must see the production to appreciate the fine way in which it has been staged, the masterful handling of the suspense, and the thoughtful work of the cast."

The New York Dramatic Mirror,
July 21, 1915.

Thomas Meighan and Charlotte Walker

Geraldine Farrar

Geraldine Farrar and
Jeanie Macpherson

CARMEN

Produced and directed by Cecil B. DeMille. Scenario by William C. de Mille, adapted from the novel by Prosper Merimée. Cameraman: Alvin Wyckoff. Film Editor: Cecil B. DeMille. Produced by the Jesse L. Lasky Feature Play Co. for release by the Paramount Pictures Corp., October 31, 1915. Five reels.

STORY

Carmen, a cigarette girl, has a fierce fight with another girl in the factory, and is put into the custody of a handsome Spanish soldier, Don José, who is infatuated with her. She entices him into letting her go free, and she runs away to join a gypsy smugglers' camp in the mountains. Don José, disgraced, follows her to the camp, but Carmen no longer has any use for him, and runs away to the city, where she quickly finds a new lover in the person of Escamillo, the new matador idol of the bullring. Don José, maddened by jealousy, follows her to the city, and stabs her to death outside the bullring.

Wallace Reid and Geraldine Farrar

CAST

Carmen	Geraldine Farrar
Don José	Wallace Reid
Escamillo	Pedro de Cordoba
Pastia	Horace B. Carpenter
Morales	Billy Elmer
Gypsy Girls	Jeanie Macpherson
	Anita King

Jeanie Macpherson,
Wallace Reid, and Geraldine Farrar

Pedro de Cordoba and
Geraldine Farrar

88

REVIEWS

"Geraldine Farrar has put her heart and soul and body into this picture, and without the aid of the magic of her voice, has proved herself one of the greatest actresses of all times. Her picture, *Carmen*, will live long after her operatic characterization has died in the limbo of forgotten singers. Her acting in this production is one of the marvels of the stage and screen, so natural, so realistic that it is hard to believe that it is acting."

The New York Dramatic Mirror,
November 6, 1915.

"One cannot do justice to *Carmen*. It is a picture of finesse, encompassing the sincere efforts of a great player—even to the point of a very rough treatment accorded the expensive person of a prima donna—of a great director and of a loyal studio support. It is not a Sunday School play, this picture of the classic heart bandit. There's a plentiful showing of emotions as they are, not as they are refined by civilization and the 'what will people say?' idea, but it is all done with a swift deftness that makes the point without the wearisome tediousness of other directors less artistic than Cecil DeMille."

Kitty Kelly in
The Chicago Tribune,
October 6, 1915.

"It is a curious commentary on the crazy economy of the theatre that a supreme dramatic soprano should give any of her precious time to a form of entertainment, to an art if you will, wherein the chief characteristic is a complete and abysmal silence. But, though the call of the movies is audible enough, there is small reason to fear that, after Miss Farrar's success, there will be a great rush of prima donnas to California, for precious few of them could so meet the exactions of the camera."

The New York Times,
November 1, 1915.

Geraldine Farrar and Wallace Reid

Victor Moore

Victor Moore

90

CHIMMIE FADDEN OUT WEST

Produced and directed by Cecil B. DeMille. Scenario also by DeMille and Jeanie Macpherson, adapted from stories by E. W. Townsend. Cameraman: Alvin Wyckoff. Film Editor: Cecil B. DeMille. Produced by the Jesse L. Lasky Feature Play Co. for release by the Paramount Pictures Corp., November 21, 1915. Five reels.

STORY

As part of a railroad publicity scheme, Chimmie Fadden is sent out to Death Valley in California with a large bag of gold nuggets, and he is then supposed to come into town with the nuggets as proof that he has made a gold strike. He is then to hire a special train to take him East, and the train is to break the transcontinental record. Matters don't turn out as planned, but Chimmie Fadden does emerge finally as a hero.

Victor Moore

CAST

Chimmie Fadden	Victor Moore
The Duchess	Camille Astor
Larry	Raymond Hatton
Mother Fadden	Mrs. Lewis McCord
Mr. Van Courtlandt	Ernest Joy
Antoine	Tom Forman
Betty Van Courtlandt	Florence Dagmar
Preston	Harry Hadfield

REVIEWS

"Here is a feature that I feel safe in praising without any 'ifs' or 'howevers.' As an actor and a

Victor Moore

laugh-producer Victor Moore is a host in himself."

W. Stephen Bush in
The Moving Picture World,
November 27, 1915.

"Victor Moore's personality is evident in all scenes of this diverting comedy. In some respects his performance in *Chimmie Fadden Out West* is better than many of his stage productions."

William Ressman Andrews in
The Motion Picture News,
December 4, 1915.

"There is a delightful combination of comedy and romance served up in the Lasky four-reeler, *Chimmie Fadden Out West*, which has just been released on the Paramount program . . . a corking comedy feature."

The Weekly Variety,
November 26, 1915.

"Though he has been given very little to work with, Victor Moore makes a thoroughly enjoyable comedy out of a picture that, owing to his inimitable manner, has many very amusing features."

The New York Dramatic Mirror,
December 4, 1915.

Victor Moore

93

Fannie Ward and Sessue Hayakawa

Sessue Hayakawa

94

Fannie Ward

THE CHEAT

Produced and directed by Cecil B. DeMille. Original scenario by Hector Turnbull. Cameraman: Alvin Wyckoff. Film Editor: Cecil B. DeMille. Produced by the Jesse L. Lasky Feature Play Co. for release by the Paramount Pictures Corp., December 12, 1915. Five reels.

STORY

Edith Hardy, a social butterfly, is treasurer of a charity, and gambles on Wall Street with the funds, in order to buy some expensive gowns she wants. The "sure tip" is a fizzle. She is frantic, and does not want to confess her indiscretion to her husband. A rich Oriental, Tori, lends her ten thousand dollars as the price of her affections. Ironically, her husband makes a killing on Wall Street and gives her that exact sum to spend as she wishes. She tries to persuade Tori to take back his money. Refusing, he calls her a cheat, and forcibly brands her naked shoulder with a Japanese symbol signifying that she is his property. Half-mad with pain, she shoots him. Her husband, appearing on the scene, assumes the guilt. Tori does not die, but Dick Hardy is found guilty of assault with intent to kill, whereupon his wife in court bares the brand on her shoulder, and confesses the truth. Tori is nearly torn apart by the furious courtroom crowd, but the Hardys are reunited.

Fannie Ward and Sessue Hayakawa

CAST

Edith Hardy	Fannie Ward
Dick Hardy	Jack Dean
Tori	Sessue Hayakawa
Jones	James Neill
Tori's Valet	Utake Abe
District Attorney	Dana Ong
Mrs. Reynolds	Hazel Childers

REVIEWS

"*The Cheat* is a mighty fine photoplay, well conceived, well written, carefully produced, and extremely well acted; melodramatic, it is true, but the kind of melodrama that is reasonable and possible, and furthermore the kind that is forceful and stirring."

The New York Dramatic Mirror,
December 25, 1915.

"Features like this one put the whole industry under obligations to the Lasky Company. On every conceivable test this picture shows a hundred per cent. Indeed, the feature is of such extraordinary merit as to call for the highest terms of praise."

W. Stephen Bush in
The Moving Picture World,
December 25, 1915.

"The picture as a feature will surely be a box-office winner, for it carries a lot of punch of 'virtue for dollars' stuff that is sure to appeal. There are some excellent lighting effects, and the work of Sessue Hayakawa is so far above the acting of Miss Ward and Jack Dean that he really should be the star in the billing for the film."

The Weekly *Variety,*
December 17, 1915.

Fannie Ward,
Utake Abe, and Sessue Hayakawa

Fannie Ward

Fannie Ward and Jack Dean

"Mr. Lasky's enthusiasm is not wholly without reason, for the picture is much above the average of its kind. But is there any more excuse for this sensational trash than for the old-fashioned melodramas in which half the characters were killed off at the end of the play? Miss Ward might learn something to help her fulfill her destiny as a great tragedienne of the screen by observing the man who acted the Japanese villain in her picture."

The New York Times,
December 13, 1915.

Horace B. Carpenter, Cleo Ridgely, and Raymond Hatton

Wallace Reid and Cleo Ridgely

98

Cleo Ridgely (*on stairs*)
and Wallace Reid

THE GOLDEN CHANCE

Produced and directed by Cecil B. DeMille. Original scenario also by DeMille and Jeannie Macpherson. Cameraman: Alvin Wyckoff. Film Editor: Cecil B. DeMille. Produced by the Jesse L. Lasky Feature Play Co. for release by the Paramount Pictures Corp., December 30, 1915. Five reels.

STORY

When Steve Denby squanders all his money on drink, his wife Mary accepts work as a seamstress from a society woman, Mrs. Hillary. Mr. Hillary is anxious to close an important business deal with an attractive young millionaire, Roger Manning, and has arranged for a social beauty to accompany Manning to a party. When the beauty is suddenly unable to appear, Mary is induced by Mrs. Hillary to substitute. Manning is fascinated by Mary's charms; but then Steve Denby chances to learn of his wife's impersonation, and tries to blackmail Manning. In a fight with the police, whom Manning has summoned, Steve Denby is killed. Manning learns who Mary really is, and more in love with her than ever, asks her to become his wife.

Wallace Reid and Cleo Ridgely

CAST

Mary Denby	Cleo Ridgely
Roger Manning	Wallace Reid
Steve Denby	Horace B. Carpenter
Mr. Hillary	Ernest Joy
Mrs. Hillary	Edythe Chapman
Jimmy, the Rat	Raymond Hatton

REVIEWS

"This is a marvelous picture. It is an ordeal for the reviewer. The gloss on all the superlatives has been worn off by the ruthless hand of the press agent, and superlatives, after all, are the only terms in which justice can be done to this picture."

W. Stephen Bush in
The Moving Picture World,
January 8, 1916.

"The master hand of Cecil B. DeMille is evident throughout the whole picture. His is the bigness of vision that can see and appreciate the value and importance of little things, and irrespective of the dramatic intensity of the story, it is the attention to seemingly inconsequential details that makes *The Golden Chance* a big, gripping, human picture. For even this story, good as it is, could have been irretrievably spoiled in the hands of a poor director. As it is, the original strength of the story is increased and accentuated, made more human and more appealing by the delicate touch of the man responsible for its production."

The New York Dramatic Mirror,
January 29, 1916.

Cleo Ridgely, Wallace Reid,
and Horace B. Carpenter.
In the background:
Edythe Chapman and Ernest Joy

100

Cleo Ridgely, Raymond Hatton, Horace B. Carpenter,
and Wallace Reid

Geraldine Farrar and Theodore Roberts

Theodore Roberts, Geraldine Farrar, and Pedro de Cordoba

Geraldine Farrar and Pedro de Cordoba

TEMPTATION

Produced and directed by Cecil B. DeMille. Original scenario by Hector Turnbull. Cameraman: Alvin Wyckoff. Film Editor: Cecil B. DeMille. Produced by the Jesse L. Lasky Feature Play Co. for release by the Paramount Pictures Corp., January 3, 1916. Six reels.

STORY

Renée Duprée is a promising but poor opera singer, very much in love with Julian, a struggling young composer. Otto Mueller, a wealthy impresario, is infatuated by Renée's charms, but she resists his advances until Julian falls desperately ill, and it is urgent that money be had at once for medical and hospital needs. Renée goes to Mueller for the money, and is tempted to sacrifice her virtue for her lover's life, but a jealous mistress kills Mueller. Renée is cleared of any complicity in the murder, and Julian and she find happiness and success.

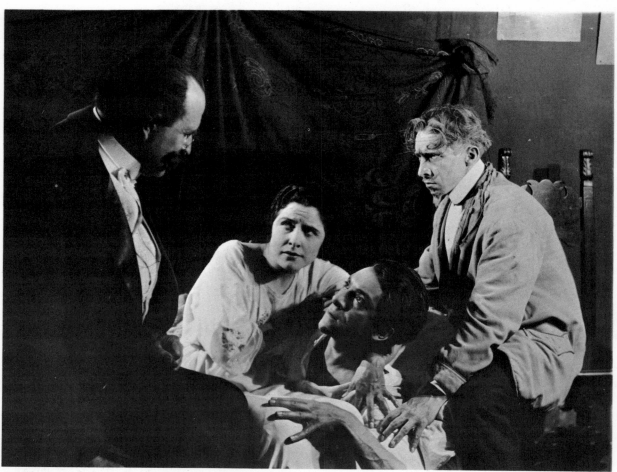

Theodore Roberts, Geraldine Farrar, Pedro de Cordoba

CAST

Renée Duprée	Geraldine Farrar
Otto Mueller	Theodore Roberts
Julian	Pedro de Cordoba
Madame Maroff	Elsie Jane Wilson
Baron Cheurial	Raymond Hatton
Opera Admirer	Sessue Hayakawa

REVIEWS

"Temptation, as resisted with the utmost propriety by Miss Geraldine Farrar, is the head and front of this Lasky feature. Miss Farrar has a personality of such magnetic charm and such vivacity that she is bound to win her audience in even a mediocre play. The same may be said for Theodore Roberts."

W. Stephen Bush in
The Moving Picture World,
January 18, 1916.

"The wonderful personality, the magnetism, and above all the inimitable histrionic power of Geraldine Farrar are brought out in this picture even more strongly than in *Carmen....*The photography is of the highest standard, and the master hand of director DeMille is discernible throughout."

The New York Dramatic Mirror,
January 8, 1916.

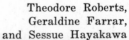

Theodore Roberts,
Geraldine Farrar,
and Sessue Hayakawa

Charlotte Walker

106

THE TRAIL OF THE LONESOME PINE

Produced and directed by Cecil B. DeMille. Scenario also by DeMille, adapted from the play by Eugene Walter and the novel by John William Fox, Jr. Cameraman: Alvin Wyckoff. Film Editor: Cecil B. DeMille. Produced by the Jesse L. Lasky Feature Play Co. for release by the Paramount Pictures Corp., February 14, 1916. Five reels.

STORY

Jack Hale, district revenue officer, is sent to the mountains of Virginia to locate a whiskey still somewhere near the Lonesome Pine Trail. He falls in love with June Tolliver, daughter of the moonshiners, and is tricked by the Tollivers, who use June as a decoy. But in the end Hale triumphs. Old Judd Tolliver destroys his still, kills the Tolliver relative who has betrayed him, and relinquishes his daughter to the trusting hands of Jack Hale.

CAST

June Tolliver	Charlotte Walker
Jack Hale	Thomas Meighan
Dave Tolliver	Earle Foxe
Judd Tolliver	Theodore Roberts
Tolliver Men	Milton Brown
	Hosea Steelman

REVIEWS

"Theodore Roberts is undoubtedly the greatest asset of this feature. His characterization of the old mountaineer was the finest piece of acting seen on any screen in many a month. Indeed, I feel tempted to doubt whether all the subtle points, all the details of his peerless impersonation can possibly be appreciated at only one view of this feature."

> W. Stephen Bush in
> *The Moving Picture World*,
> February 26, 1916.

"Cecil B. DeMille has made a truly artistic picture out of the now famous story and play of John Fox, Jr. It might be described as a picture of the 'better sort.' He has had the best of material to work with in story, drama and cast, and he has overlooked no opportunities, so far as we can see, to provide telling situations, and 'punch'—if we may be allowed to coin a phrase!"

> Harry F. Thew in
> *The Motion Picture News*,
> February 26, 1916.

"It is a remarkable motion picture reproduction of the play which Eugene Walter adapted from the novel by John Fox....*The Trail of the Lonesome Pine* is a corking story exceedingly well told in pictures."

> The Weekly *Variety*,
> February 11, 1916.

Theodore Roberts,
Thomas Meighan, and Charlotte Walker

Charlotte Walker and Earle Foxe

Theodore Roberts

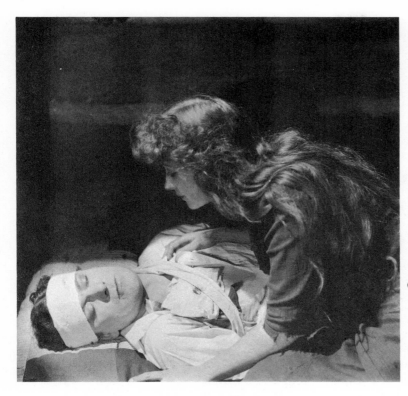

Charlotte Walker and Thomas Meighan

Charlotte Walker and Thomas Meighan

Elliott Dexter and Marie Doro

DeMille and Marie Doro

THE HEART OF NORA FLYNN

Produced and directed by Cecil B. DeMille. Scenario by Jeanie Macpherson, adapted from a story by Hector Turnbull. Cameraman: Alvin Wyckoff. Film Editor: Cecil B. DeMille. Produced by the Jesse L. Lasky Feature Play Co. for release by the Paramount Pictures Corp., April 23, 1916. Five reels.

STORY

Nora Flynn, a nursemaid in a wealthy home, loves the chauffeur, Nolan. Nora protects her mistress, Mrs. Stone, from being caught when Mrs. Stone foolishly tries to run away with a man-about-town, and hides Mrs. Stone's lover in her own room, where the jealous Nolan discovers and shoots him. Although the lover is not killed, there is a newspaper scandal, and Mr. Stone dismisses Nora as being unfit to supervise the education of his children. Nora refuses to inform upon her mistress, who, however, does tell Nolan the truth, and Nora and he are reunited.

111

Marie Doro and Elliot Dexter

Elliott Dexter and Marie Doro

CAST

Nora Flynn	Marie Doro
Nolan	Elliott Dexter
Brantley Stone	Ernest Joy
Mrs. Stone	Lola May
Tommy Stone	Billy Jacobs
Jack Murray	Charles West
Anne Stone	Peggy George
Maggie, the Cook	Mrs. Lewis McCord

REVIEWS

"This feature reaches the best Lasky standards. In the first place, a real human interest story is there. It is entirely original. It illustrates one of the most admirable traits in the Irish character. A man or a woman with a real Irish heart cannot betray a confidence. Nothing is more repellent to the Irish character than to be an 'informer.' "

W. Stephen Bush in
The Moving Picture World,
May 6, 1916.

"Marie Doro repeats and accentuates her previous screen successes in this offering. From start to finish it is her winning personality that excites and holds the sympathy of the audience, and while Hector Turnbull has written a good strong story, and the scenario writer and director have filled it to overflowing with delightful human touches, still when all is said and done, it is Marie Doro who carries away the laurels of the production. . . . The picture was staged in the usual DeMille manner, with the right kind of settings and exceedingly beautiful photographic and lighting effects."

The New York Dramatic Mirror,
April 29, 1916.

Marie Doro and Lola May

Wallace Reid and Geraldine Farrar

114

Geraldine Farrar, Anita King,
Ernest Joy, and Pedro de Cordoba

MARIA ROSA

Produced and directed by Cecil B. DeMille. Scenario by William C. de Mille, adapted from the play by Wallace Gilpatrick and Guido Marburg, which was translated and adapted from an original play by Angel Guimera. Cameraman: Alvin Wyckoff. Film Editor: Cecil B. DeMille. Produced by the Jesse L. Lasky Feature Play Co. for release by the Paramount Pictures Corp., May 7, 1916. Five reels.

STORY

Maria Rosa, a Catalonian peasant, is loved by both Andreas, a vintner, and his supposed friend, Ramon. In a fight Ramon kills his opponent, Pedro, a fisherman, using a knife belonging to Andreas, who is convicted of the murder and sent to prison for ten years. Maria Rosa, loving Andreas, swears to wait for him, but Ramon manages to make her believe that Andreas has died in prison, and she agrees to marry Ramon.

On their wedding day Andreas returns, having been paroled from prison for performing a brave deed during a revolt. When Maria Rosa learns the truth, she stabs Ramon to death, but before he dies Ramon tells the priest that he himself accidentally fell upon his knife, thus vindicating his treachery and leaving the way open for Maria Rosa and Andreas to wed.

115

Geraldine Farrar and Wallace Reid

CAST

Maria Rosa	Geraldine Farrar
Andreas	Wallace Reid
Ramon	Pedro de Cordoba
The Priest	James Neill
Carlos	Ernest Joy
Pedro	Horace B. Carpenter
Ana, Carlos' wife	Anita King

REVIEWS

"Having seen Geraldine Farrar in all her great roles, both on the singing and on the silent stage, I have no hesitation whatever in saying that in the part of Maria Rosa she has reached her greatest histrionic triumph."

W. Stephen Bush in
The Moving Picture World,
May 13, 1916.

"The manner of the telling makes this old story of the triangle seem new. Its mountings, settings and acting are sufficient to make it distinctly a 'worthwhile' picture, and its star, Geraldine Farrar, is a guarantee of box-office quality."

Harvey F. Thew in
The Motion Picture News,
May 13, 1916.

Geraldine Farrar and Pedro de Cordoba

"Cecil B. DeMille's direction throughout the whole production is without fault. He has brought his story out in a clear, convincing manner, and has achieved a fade-in scene for his emotional climax that is one of the best we have ever seen produced."

The New York Dramatic Mirror,
May 6, 1916.

Pedro de Cordoba,
Horace B. Carpenter, Wallace Reid,
and Geraldine Farrar

Pedro de Cordoba and Geraldine Farrar

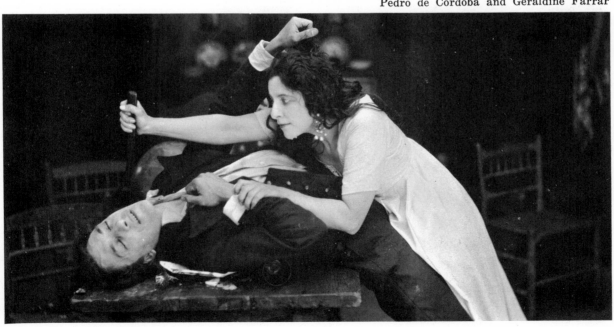

117

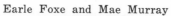
Earle Foxe and Mae Murray

118

THE DREAM GIRL

Produced and directed by Cecil B. DeMille. Original scenario by Jeanie Macpherson. Cameraman: Alvin Wyckoff. Film Edior: Cecil B. DeMille. Produced by the Jesse L. Lasky Feature Play Co. for release by the Paramount Pictures Corp., July 27, 1916. Five reels.

STORY

Meg, a waif of the San Francisco docks, takes refuge from the ugly world of reality in a dream world of her own making, believing she will be rescued from the sordidness of her life by a true Galahad. Her father operates a "social club," where liquor is sold illegally, and he contrives with a crony known as "English" Hal, supplying him with funds so that he can impersonate an English nobleman and win the heart of a rich young girl. But Meg, rescued from her environment by a Detention Squad, is put on probation to Benjamin Merton, wealthy father of the very girl Jim Dugan and "English" Hal have contrived to compromise and blackmail. Meg finds her real-life Galahad in the person of Merton's son Tom, but when she discovers her father's and "English" Hal's nefarious plan, she exposes them, and tearfully prepares to leave her new home. But the Mertons persuade her to remain, especially young Tom Merton, who loves and wants to marry her.

CAST

Meg Dugan	Mae Murray
Jim Dugan	Theodore Roberts
Tom Merton	Earle Foxe
Benjamin Merton	James Neill
"English" Hal	Charles West
Alice Merton	Mary Mersch
Character Woman	Mrs. Lewis McCord

REVIEWS

"Because it is well done, rather than because of any extraordinary quality in the story, *The Dream Girl* belongs among the good,. if not the best of the Lasky pictures. If there were any doubts about the wisdom of starring Mae Murray after her performances in *To Have and To Hold* and *Sweet Kitty Bellairs*, they are set at rest by her playing of a slum girl in this photoplay, from the pen of Jeanie Macpherson and produced by Cecil B. DeMille."

Lynde Denig in
The Moving Picture World,
July 29, 1916.

"The material is handled skillfully by Mr. DeMille to create heart interest, some humor of character, and a strain of mystery. The settings and locations, of course, are excellent, the continuity fine, and the suspense fair."

Oscar Cooper in
The Motion Picture News,
July 29, 1916.

Theodore Roberts, Mae Murray, and Charles West

Mae Murray and Earle Foxe

Mae Murray, Earle Foxe, and Theodore Roberts

Geraldine Farrar

Geraldine Farrar,
Tully Marshall,
and Theodore Roberts

122

Geraldine Farrar

JOAN THE WOMAN

Produced and directed by Cecil B. DeMille. Scenario by Jeanie Macpherson. Cameraman: Alvin Wyckoff. Film Editor: Cecil B. DeMille. Music Score: William Furst. Exploited by the Cardinal Film Co. for release by the Paramount Pictures Corp., January 4, 1917. Ten reels.

STORY

The story opens in the trenches of World War I. An English officer, Eric Trent, has been ordered to go on a mission from which he cannot hope to return alive. He is inspired to go on the mission by a vision of Joan of Arc, who appears to him when he finds the decayed sword she had once used; he is inspired by her to fulfill the mission in order to expiate his sin against her centuries previously. The story fades back to the historical account of Joan leading the French Army to victory, her betrayal to the Burgundians by the English soldier who loves her, Eric Trent, and climaxes with the trial of Joan and her subsequent burning at the stake.

CAST

Joan of Arc	Geraldine Farrar
Charles VIII, *King of France*	Raymond Hatton
General La Hire	Hobart Bosworth
Cauchon	Theodore Roberts
Eric Trent	Wallace Reid
La Tremouille, *King's Advisor*	Charles Clary
Laxart	James Neill
L'Oiseleur, the Mad Monk	Tully Marshall
Gaspard	Lawrence Peyton
Jacques d'Arc	Horace B. Carpenter
The King's Favorite	Cleo Ridgely
Isambeau	Lillian Leighton
Katherine	Marjorie Daw
Pierre	Stephen Gray
Robert de Beaudricourt	Ernest Joy
Jean de Metz	John Oaker
The Duke of Burgundy	Hugo B. Koch
John of Luxembourg	William Conklin
The Executioner	Walter Long
Guy Townes	Billy Elmer
Michael	Emilius Jorgensen
Starving Peasant	Ramon Samaniegos (Novarro)

REVIEWS

"If anything in the way of evidence were needed to convince the photoplay-going public that Cecil B. DeMille belongs in the front rank of the day, his direction of *Joan the Woman* should supply it in full measure."

George Blaisdell in
The Moving Picture World,
January 13, 1917.

"*Joan the Woman* is a triumph for Geraldine Farrar, but equally as much is it a triumph for Cecil DeMille, its producer. Through his long picture he has interpolated the personal and the spectacular veins of interest with the fine result of dramatic contrast."

Peter Milne in
The Motion Picture News,
January 6, 1917.

"Producer DeMille has given us some wonderfully effective battle scenes and has presented an atmosphere of distinction in his dramatic moments which, combined with the dynamic personalities of the star and supporting cast, has made all of the dramatic moments truly impressive. There is an air of distinction and class about the entire production which places it in the front rank of big productions, and certainly no one can see this offering without being impressed with the tremendous strides made in the last two or three years by our producers of big films."

Wid's,
January 4, 1917.

"It is impossible to describe in detail what producer DeMille accomplished with such a wealth of material. Suffice it to say that no one else could have done more and few, if any, could have done as much."

The Weekly *Variety,*
December 29, 1916.

Geraldine Farrar

Wallace Reid
and Geraldine Farrar

Geraldine Farrar, Wallace Reid, and players

Geraldine Farrar and Wallace Reid

126

Raymond Hatton and Geraldine Farrar

(*Opposite page*) Mary Pickford

Mary Pickford and Charles Ogle

ROMANCE OF THE REDWOODS

Produced and directed by Cecil B. DeMille. Scenario also by DeMille and Jeanie Macpherson. Cameraman: Alvin Wyckoff. Film Editor: Cecil B. DeMille. Produced by Artcraft Pictures Corp. for release by the Paramount Pictures Corp., May 14, 1917. Eight reels.

STORY

Arriving in the West from her New England home, Jenny Lawrence is welcomed by a road agent assuming the identity of her uncle, who has been killed. Forced to live with him as his niece, she falls in love with him, and when he is caught trying to rob the stagecoach on his one last hold-up job, Jenny pretends that he is the father of the child she carries in her arms. Not until the sheriff's posse lets the lovers go free is it discovered that the "baby" is really a doll.

Elliott Dexter and Mary Pickford

Mary Pickford

REVIEWS

"Naturally does the picture show the results of Mr. DeMille's direction, but where his work as author ends and his services as director begin is unknown. At any rate, he has gotten the most from his players, has handled every scene effectively."

Peter Milne in
The Motion Picture News,
May 26, 1917.

"A story of the rush to California for gold in '49, it moves along conventional but well-defined lines that give the star many effective moments in a character skillfully adapted to her personality. At the finish it introduces a situation that will please many of Miss Pickford's admirers immensely; others will regret its use in a picture with which she is connected."

Edward Weitzel in
The Moving Picture World,
May 26, 1917.

Walter Long, Mary Pickford, and Elliott Dexter

Mary Pickford

Jack Holt and Mary Pickford

132

Mary Pickford

THE LITTLE AMERICAN

Produced and directed by Cecil B. DeMille. Scenario also by DeMille and Jeanie Macpherson, adapted from a story by Miss Macpherson. Cameraman: Alvin Wyckoff. Film Editor: Cecil B. DeMille. Produced by Artcraft Pictures Corp. for release by the Paramount Pictures Corp., July 12, 1917. Six reels.

STORY

Karl Von Austreim, a German-American living in the United States, is ordered back to Germany to join his regiment, as is a French-American, Count Jules de Destin. Both are in love with an American girl, Angela Moore, and subsequently Angela sails for France on a ship which is torpedoed by a German submarine. Angela is rescued and gets to France, only to find her aunt dead and the family chateau transformed into a hospital. The German forces arrive, and Angela is attacked and nearly raped in the dark by a man she discovers to be Karl Von Austreim. She forgives him, but when she is discovered sending secret messages over the telephone to the French Count de Destin, she is ordered shot, as is Karl when he comes to her defense and defames the

DeMille, Mary Pickford, and cast

Mary Pickford

Jack Holt,
Mary Pickford, and Wallace Beery

134

Fatherland. Both are saved from execution by the French attack, but Karl is killed in the crossfire, and it is Count de Destin who returns to America with Angela.

CAST

Angela Moore	Mary Pickford
Karl Von Austreim	Jack Holt
German Commander	Hobart Bosworth
Count Jules de Destin	Raymond Hatton
German Captain	Walter Long

Other Players: James Neill, Ben Alexander, Guy Oliver, Edythe Chapman, Lillian Leighton, Norman Kerry, Wallace Beery, Gordon Griffith, Ramon Novarro, Sam Wood, Colleen Moore.

REVIEWS

"Technically, Mr. DeMille has again demonstrated his ability to register effective scenes. I believe, however, that he has seriously erred in his choice of story material and his elaboration of certain details."

Wid's,
July 12, 1917.

"As a patriotic spectacle and as an ideal Pickford vehicle, *The Little American* is superb. When the German hero denounces the Emperor and the system that once was his with a ferocious 'damn' in order to protect Angela Moore, the Little American, and when Angela announces that she has quit being neutral and has turned human; then are the times for loud applause. But there is more than stirring speeches and patriotic flag waving to *The Little American*."

Peter Milne in
The Motion Picture News,
July 21, 1917.

Mary Pickford

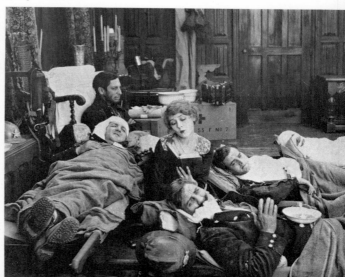

Mary Pickford

Mary Pickford and Jack Holt

Geraldine Farrar and Wallace Reid

THE WOMAN GOD FORGOT

Produced and directed by Cecil B. DeMille. Original scenario by Jeanie Macpherson. Cameraman: Alvin Wyckoff. Film Editor: Cecil B. DeMille. Produced by Artcraft Pictures Corp. for release by the Paramount Pictures Corp., November 8, 1917. Six reels.

STORY

When Cortez lands in Mexico, he sends Captain Alvarado to Montezuma with a message to surrender. Montezuma casts Alvarado into a dungeon, but Tecza, Montezuma's daughter, has fallen in love with Alvarado, and rescues him. The warrior, Guatemoco, loves Tecza, and discovering Alvarado hidden in her chambers, he takes him captive. Tecza is promised as wife to Guatemoco, and Alvarado is to be offered to the gods as a sacrifice. In the middle of the night Tecza goes secretly to the camp of Cortez and leads him and his Spanish warriors back inside the city. Alvarado is saved, but the entire Aztec nation is destroyed. Tecza, bitter, retires to a distant valley to mourn, and she is found there by Alvarado, who convinces her of his true love.

CAST

Tecza, daughter of Montezuma	Geraldine Farrar
Alvarado	Wallace Reid
Montezuma	Raymond Hatton
Cortez	Hobart Bosworth
Guatemoco	Theodore Kosloff
Taloc, high priest	Walter Long
Tecza's Handmaiden	Julia Faye
Aztec Woman	Olga Grey

REVIEWS

"To the student of history the accuracy of the exteriors, interiors, costumes and accessories in *The Woman God Forgot*, the Artcraft production starring Geraldine Farrar, will make strong appeal. To the casual amusement seeker the abbreviated tale of the clash between the highest civilization of the new world and that of the old, with the consequent destruction of the former, will prove equally absorbing."

E. T. Keyser in
The Moving Picture World,
November 17, 1917.

"Miss Macpherson's scenario provided Mr. DeMille with wonderful opportunities to exercise his art in obtaining spectacular effects, and while these plainly dominate the picture, the personal interest has by no means been neglected."

Peter Milne in
The Motion Picture News,
November 17, 1917.

Wallace Reid and Geraldine Farrar

Wallace Reid, Geraldine Farrar, and Theodore Kosloff

138

Wallace Reid

139

Geraldine Farrar

Tully Marshall
and Geraldine Farrar

140

Geraldine Farrar

THE DEVIL STONE

Produced and directed by Cecil B. DeMille. Scenario by Jeanie Macpherson, adapted from a story by Beatrice DeMille and Leighton Osmun. Cameraman: Alvin Wyckoff. Film Editor: Cecil B. DeMille. Produced by Artcraft Pictures Corp. for release by the Paramount Pictures Corp., December 31, 1917. Six reels.

STORY

Marcia Manot, a Breton fishermaid, finds on the seashore a rare emerald, once the property of a long-ago Norse Queen. It is believed that whoever possesses the stone is accursed; nevertheless, Silas Martin, a venal old American, coveting the emerald, persuades Marcia to become his wife, and so gains possession of it. She learns that he has married her only to compromise her with his business manager, Guy Sterling, and so gain a divorce. In an effort to regain the emerald, Marcia quarrels and fights with her husband and accidentally kills him. She weds Sterling, and when a detective learns the truth about Silas Martin's death, he advises her to return the stone to a priest in a Breton chapel. The curse is lifted; the detective does not prosecute her; and Marcia and Sterling find new happiness together.

141

Geraldine Farrar and players

CAST

Marcia Manot	Geraldine Farrar
Guy Sterling	Wallace Reid
Silas Martin	Tully Marshall
Robert Judson	Hobart Bosworth

Other Players: Mabel Van Buren, Lillian Leighton, Horace B. Carpenter, Ernest Joy, James Neill, Gustav von Seyffertitz, Burwell Mamrick.

REVIEWS

"From the angles of artistry of production and photography it is excellent, as indeed are the great majority of the pictures made at the Lasky

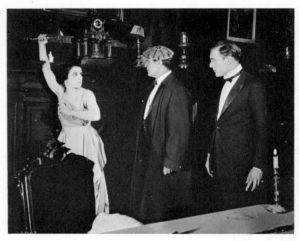

Geraldine Farrar,
Hobart Bosworth, and Wallace Reid

Geraldine Farrar and Tully Marshall

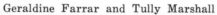

Studio. The introduction of the theme of superstition throws something of a weird atmosphere over the story at times, which is of material assistance in bolstering the interest up to a point above the average."

Peter Milne in
The Motion Picture News,
January 5, 1918.

"The story of *The Devil Stone* is calculated to boom and roar with creeps, quakes and superstition—signs of witchcraft and the traditional goblins—with a big emerald playing an important part all the way.... Allowing for suppositions and certain stretches of the imagination, the picture will interest and entertain."

The Weekly *Variety*,
December 21, 1917.

Wallace Reid and Geraldine Farrar

Elliott Dexter and Kathlyn Williams

144

Kathlyn Williams

THE WHISPERING CHORUS

Produced and directed by Cecil B. DeMille. Scenario by Jeanie Macpherson, adapted from a novel by Perley Poore Sheehan. Cameraman: Alvin Wyckoff. Film Editor: Cecil B. DeMille. Produced by Artcraft Pictures Corp. for release by Famous Players-Lasky Corp. on the Paramount Program, March 28, 1918. Six reels.

STORY

John Trimble has embezzled funds, and desiring to assume a second identity, he arranges to have a mutilated body buried as his own. But some years later he is arrested and put on trial as the murderer of himself. At his trial, he goes unrecognized except by his own mother, who dies of the shock. But his mother, before expiring, begs him not to reveal his true identity, as his wife has married the Governor of the state and is about to become a mother. The truth will create a ruinous scandal and make her unborn child illegitimate. Trimble accepts his fate and goes to his death, maintaining the secret of his true identity.

Raymond Hatton

Noah Beery and Raymond Hatton

Raymond Hatton

CAST

John Trimble	Raymond Hatton
Jane Trimble	Kathlyn Williams
John Trimble's Mother	Edythe Chapman
George Coggeswell	Elliott Dexter
Longshoreman	Noah Beery
Chief McFarland	Guy Oliver
Charles Barden	John Burton
Tom Burns	J. Parke Jones
F. P. Clumley	Tully Marshall
Stauberry	W. H. Brown
Channing	James Neill
Mocking Face	Gustav von Seyffertitz
Evil Face	Walter Lynch
Good Face	Edna Mae Cooper
Girl in Waterfront Dive	Julia Faye

REVIEWS

"Screen the bare plot of Cecil B. DeMille's latest offering and we have bold, gruesome, over-wrought melodrama; add the artistic touch-es—the double exposures, punchful titles, pictur-esque setting and vivid character-drawing—and we have one of the most bizarre, fanciful and powerful photodramas of the year."

"E.M.L." in
The Motion Picture Magazine,
July, 1918.

"*The Whispering Chorus* is intended to represent the small voices and thoughts of the average mind that work for good and evil. The thought is a good one for the purpose of picturization and the manner in which it is worked out interests. The usual tricks of double exposure are employed in setting the story on the screen, but they are not worked to death."

The Weekly *Variety*,
March 29, 1918.

Raymond Hatton and Julia Faye

Edythe Chapman
and Ethel Wales

147

In background: Marcia Manon, Julia Faye,
Alice Taafe (Terry), and Theodore Roberts

Florence Vidor

OLD WIVES FOR NEW

Produced and directed by Cecil B. DeMille. Scenario by Jeanie Macpherson, based on the novel by David Graham Phillips. Cameraman: Alvin Wyckoff. Film Editor: Cecil B. DeMille. Produced by Artcraft Pictures Corp. for release by Famous Players-Lasky Corp. on the Paramount Program, May 20, 1918. Six reels.

STORY

Charles Murdock has married in haste and in later years neglects his wife, who grows fat and lazy. Murdock falls in love with Juliet Raeburn, a younger and charming woman, but when a murder is committed and Juliet's name is involved, Murdock, who is now free to remarry, leaves Juliet to marry another woman, Viola, whom he takes to Paris. Viola divorces him to wed his secretary. Juliet re-encounters Murdock abroad, and they are reunited.

CAST

Charles Murdock	Elliott Dexter
Juliet Raeburn	Florence Vidor
Sophy Murdock	Sylvia Ashton
Sophy (in the prologue)	Wanda Hawley
Berkeley	Theodore Roberts
Norma Murdock	Helen Jerome Eddy
Viola	Marcia Manon
Jessie	Julia Faye
Charley Murdock	J. Parke Jones
Bertha	Edna Mae Cooper
Blagden	Gustav von Seyffertitz
Simcox	Tully Marshall
Maid	Lillian Leighton
Housekeeper	Maym Kelso
Saleslady	Alice Taafe (Terry)

REVIEWS

"It is a remarkable picture and as a picture it has been given an equally remarkable production by Cecil B. DeMille. There are somewhat risqué situations in the story, but these have been handled delicately. It is not a story that children will understand, and it is one that the prudes will consider a reflection on themselves. All in all, it is one of the most satisfactory pictures that has been shown on Broadway in months."

R. E. Pritchard in
The Motion Picture News,
June 8, 1918.

"In adapting David Graham Phillips' brilliant novel, *Old Wives for New,* to the screen, Cecil B. DeMille, the star Lasky director, accomplished an admirable product. It is fortunate that the picturization fell into such expert hands. The results might have been fated otherwise, for there is a mixing of the fictional with the real."

The Weekly *Variety,*
May 24, 1918.

Elliott Dexter and Florence Vidor

Gustav Von Seyffertitz and Sylvia Ashton

Florence Vidor
and Elliott Dexter

Florence Vidor, Marcia Manon,
Julia Faye, Alice Taafe (Terry),
and Theodore Roberts

Wanda Hawley and Elliott Dexter with extras

Elliott Dexter and Kathlyn Williams

WE CAN'T HAVE EVERYTHING

Produced and directed by Cecil B. DeMille. Scenario by William C. de Mille, adapted from the novel by Rupert Hughes. Cameraman: Alvin Wyckoff. Film Editors: Cecil B. DeMille & Anne Bauchens. Produced by Artcraft Pictures Corp. for release by Famous Players-Lasky Corp. on the Paramount Program, July 7, 1918. Six reels.

STORY

Charity Cheever, a society woman, is neglected by her millionaire husband, who is having an affair with a dancer, Zada L'Etoile. Charity is secretly loved by Jim Dyckman, a rejected suitor, but she advises him to forget her and marry a nice girl. Unfortunately, Dyckman picks out a blonde "baby vamp," Kedzie Thropp, and is beguiled into marriage. Meanwhile, Charity has gained sufficient evidence to divorce her husband, and learns thereafter to her regret that Jim Dyckman is no longer available. But Kedzie is bored with being Mrs. Dyckman and wants to marry the Marquis of Strathdene. Kedzie is able to divorce Dyckman, naming Charity as the other woman, and Charity and Dyckman go abroad, where they are quietly married, while the Marquis weds Kedzie before he rejoins his regiment. When Kedzie laments that their honeymoon is being spoiled, he reminds her that "we can't have everything."

153

CAST

Charity Coe Cheever	Kathlyn Williams
Jim Dyckman	Elliott Dexter
Kedzie Thropp	Wanda Hawley
Zada L'Etoile	Sylvia Breamer
Peter Cheever	Thurston Hall
Marquis of Strathdene	Raymond Hatton
The Director	Tully Marshall
The Sultan	Theodore Roberts
Detective	James Neill
Heavy	Ernest Joy
Props	Billy Elmer
Kedzie's Father	Charles Ogle
Kedzie's Mother	Sylvia Ashton

REVIEWS

"Mr. DeMille is certainly on the right track to bring out this kind of story, enlightening people who are content to regard the whole subject rather superficially, as he is in typing the story with interesting people, rather than producing dull vehicles, to exploit some exacting star of limited histrionic ability. His visualizations have an added charm in their beautiful appeal to the senses—they reach thought and judgment through sentiment. He has taken a group of selfish and self-indulgent people in easy circumstances and clearly set forth their lack of fine sentiment and higher morality by methods so subtle that the motive is felt rather than seen."

Louis Reeves Harrison in
The Moving Picture World,
July 20, 1918.

"Imagine the proceedings at a divorce court recounted by a skilled novelist with a highly developed bump of satire and not a little sense of humor instead of by a journalist and you gain a faint idea of the character of Cecil DeMille's latest production, *We Can't Have Everything.*"

Peter Milne in
The Motion Picture News,
July 20, 1918.

Wanda Hawley, Theodore Roberts, and Tully Marshall

"The most pretentious of the feature photoplays presented at the leading moving picture
theatres this week is Cecil B. DeMille's *We Can't
Have Everything*, and in many ways the production is above the average, but its merit lies more
in separate scenes and individual accomplish-
ments by director, actors, and camera than in the
play as a whole. The scene of a burning moving
picture studio, for example—which is said to
have been made possible by the opportune fire at
the Lasky Studio in California—is remarkable,
both for the staged confusion of the studio
people and the many entertaining scenes concerned with the making of a movie....Also, the
capable hand and eye of Mr. DeMille are evident
throughout the picture."

The New York Times,
July 15, 1918.

Kathlyn Williams and Elliott Dexter

Bryant Washburn (*standing*)

G. Butler Clonbough
and Bryant Washburn

Bryant Washburn and Florence Vidor

TILL I COME BACK TO YOU

Produced and directed by Cecil B. DeMille. Original scenario by Jeanie Macpherson. Cameraman: Alvin Wyckoff. Film Editor: Anne Bauchens. Presented by Jesse L. Lasky for Artcraft Pictures Corp., released by Famous Players-Lasky on the Paramount Program, September 1, 1918. Six reels.

STORY

Yvonne, a beautiful Belgian girl, has married Karl Von Krutz, a German. When war breaks out, Von Krutz admits to his wife that he is a spy and joins the German forces. When the United States enters the conflict, Captain Jefferson Strong assumes the identity and papers of Von Krutz, and is ordered to enter the German territory and destroy a liquid fire base. But when the time comes, he is forced to cut the wires and avert an explosion in order to save the lives of Yvonne and sixty-five young war orphans for whom she is caring. He is tried at court martial, but freed by order of the Belgian King Albert. When Von Krutz dies, Yvonne and Captain Strong are married.

Florence Vidor and Bryant Washburn

Bryant Washburn and Florence Vidor

Bryant Washburn and Monte Blue

CAST

Captain Jefferson Strong	Bryant Washburn
Yvonne	Florence Vidor
Karl Von Krutz	G. Butler Clonbough
King Albert of Belgium	Winter Hall
Jacques	George E. Stone
Susette	Julia Faye
Margot	Lillian Leighton
U.S. Colonel	Clarence Geldart
Rosa	May Giracci
Rosa's Father	C. Renfeld
Stroheim	W. J. Irving
Hans	F. Butterworth
American Doughboy	Monte Blue

REVIEWS

"Mr. DeMille's handling of this production is thorough in detail and beautiful in its broad effects. He has also exercised rare judgment in eliminating the useless, preserving only what augments interest from start to finish. Even exaggerations become plausible under such artistic handling, and he deserves high praise for sticking to his progressive principles, not trying to empty our moving picture theatres with outworn imitations and repeats that are without reason for thoroughly modern presentation. He may be only trying out a new policy of giving the audience fresh fruit instead of the decayed kind, but he is on the right track. More such honest productions will fill to overflowing those theatres now suffering a loss of business laid to 'war times.' Congratulations, Mr. DeMille."

Louis Reeves Harrison in
The Moving Picture World,
September 7, 1918.

"There are few directors in this country who have Mr. DeMille's ability to make pictures. He knows what the camera can do, and how to make it do its best. *Till I Come Back to You* reveals his power in a succession of amusing, beautiful, vivid pictures that would make any photoplay worth seeing."

The New York Times,
August 26, 1918.

Monte Blue, Bryant Washburn, and allied soldiers

Florence Vidor and Bryant Washburn

Theodore Roberts, Charles Ogle,
Elliott Dexter, and Ann Little

Jack Holt and Elliott Dexter

Katherine MacDonald, Elliott Dexter,
and Ann Little

Jack Holt, Theodore Roberts, and Monte Blue

160

Ann Little and Katherine MacDonald

Katherine MacDonald,
Elliott Dexter, and Pat Moore

THE SQUAW MAN

Directed by Cecil B. DeMille. Scenario by Beulah Marie Dix, adapted from the play by Edwin Milton Royle. Cameraman: Alvin Wyckoff. Editor: Anne Bauchens. Presented by Jesse L. Lasky for Artcraft Pictures Corp., released by Famous Players Lasky Corp. on the Paramount Program, December 15, 1918. Six reels.

STORY

The story of this first re-make of *The Squaw Man* remained substantially the same as that first made by DeMille and released in 1914.

Katherine MacDonald

Jack Holt and Elliott Dexter

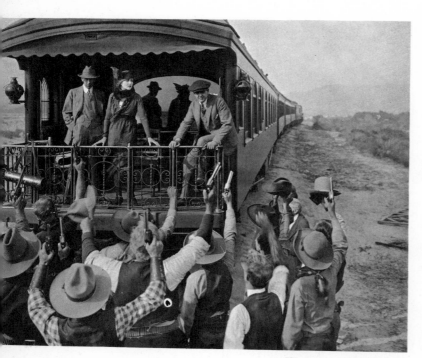

Katherine MacDonald

Jack Holt

162

"The present picture was made under the direction of Cecil B. DeMille and is a reproduction of the photoplay which he produced four years ago.... Technically the picture leaves little to be desired."

The Weekly *Variety*,
November 8, 1918.

"As a production—intelligent, finely disposed as to locations, correct as to customs and interiors, deliberate and logical as to development of story—this marks Cecil DeMille at his best."

Julian Johnson in
Photoplay Magazine,
February, 1919.

Elliott Dexter and Jack Holt

The charity bazaar

Gloria Swanson

Gloria Swanson

164

Lew Cody and Gloria Swanson

DON'T CHANGE YOUR HUSBAND

Directed by Cecil B. DeMille. Original scenario by Jeanie Macpherson. Cameraman: Alvin Wyckoff. Film Editor: Anne Bauchens. Presented by Jesse L. Lasky for Artcraft Pictures Corp., released by Famous Players-Lasky Corp. on the Paramount Program, January 26, 1919. Six reels.

STORY

Leila Porter wearies of her prosaic, newly-rich husband, a glue king who is forever eating green onions and is very careless about his personal appearance. She divorces him, and marries an attentive playboy, Schuyler Van Sutphen, but when she discovers what a two-timing wolf Van Sutphen is, she is only too happy to divorce him and remarry her now-reformed first husband.

165

CAST

James Denby Porter	Elliott Dexter
Leila Porter	Gloria Swanson
Schuyler Van Sutphen	Lew Cody
Mrs. Huckney	Sylvia Ashton
The Bishop	Theodore Roberts
Nanette	Julia Faye
Butler	James Neill
Faun	Ted Shawn

Gloria Swanson

166

REVIEWS

"Cecil B. DeMille's share of the work accounts for the artistic excellence of the production. He is to be commended for helping the screen to develop a little-used form of comedy, and for giving the picture his best endeavors."

Edward Weitzel in
The Moving Picture World,
February 8, 1919.

"This picture possesses all the earmarks of success. The story is clean and interesting and, as it has been handled with the usual care that marks all DeMille's contributions, it should give universal satisfaction."

P. S. Harrison in
The Motion Picture News,
February 8, 1919.

"This enterprise, as a matter of screen tone and wall decoration, is a masterpiece. As a story, it starts a masterpiece and ends a masterflop. Had Miss Macpherson, who conceived the entanglements, kept pace with Mr. DeMille, who visibly unwound them, this piece would certainly have been the first great and true society play born on the screen. The DeMille faculty of exquisite detail is in its dazzling zenith. Here is life—just as life springs up and grows in gardens fertilized with gold."

Julian Johnson in
Photoplay Magazine,
April, 1919.

"Cecil B. DeMille's latest Artcraft release written by Jeanie Macpherson bears the hallmark of a high-class picture. Clean and wholesome, sustained in interest, it makes a double-edged appeal. It touches home both man and woman, and in thus doing Mr. DeMille has assured a success for his really fine work."

The Weekly *Variety*,
February 7, 1919.

Lew Cody and Gloria Swanson

Lew Cody, Gloria Swanson, and Elliott Dexter

167

Gloria Swanson and Ted Shawn

Gloria Swanson and Sylvia Ashton

Gloria Swanson and Wanda Hawley

FOR BETTER, FOR WORSE

Produced and directed by Cecil B. DeMille. Scenario by Jeanie Macpherson, based upon the adaptation by William C. de Mille of the play by Edgar Selwyn. Cameraman: Alvin Wyckoff. Editor: Anne Bauchens. Presented by Jesse L. Lasky for Artcraft Pictures Corp., released by Famous Players-Lasky Corp. on the Paramount Program, May 4, 1919. Seven reels.

STORY

Dr. Edward Meade and his friend, Richard Burton, are both rivals for the hand of Sylvia Norcross, who favors Dr. Meade. Both men have enlisted in the service, but at the last minute, Dr. Meade is asked by the head surgeon of the children's hospital to stay at home and attend to the ill and deformed children under his care. Sylvia, however, believes Meade to be a slacker, and marries Burton before he sails for the war overseas. Sylvia later learns the truth of Dr. Meade's sacrifice in staying home, and falls in love with him. When she learns that Burton has been killed in battle, she consents to wed Dr. Meade. But on their wedding day, Burton returns home; he had been maimed and brutally scarred, but plastic surgery has partially restored him. Meade and

Gloria Swanson, Elliott Dexter, and players

Sylvia agree that Burton has the right to remain her husband, but Burton sees that Sylvia is secretly repulsed by his injuries. Burton finds happiness with another girl, Betty Hoyt, and after a divorce Sylvia and Dr. Meade marry.

CAST

Dr. Edward Meade	Elliott Dexter
Richard Burton	Tom Forman
Sylvia Norcross	Gloria Swanson
Sylvia's Aunt	Sylvia Ashton
Bud	Raymond Hatton
Hospital Head	Theodore Roberts
Betty Hoyt	Wanda Hawley
Doctor	Winter Hall
Crusader	Jack Holt
Colonial Soldier	Fred Huntley

REVIEWS

"Up to the minute in theme, dignified in tone, adroitly proportioned and correctly presenting a collection of human beings that interest by their sterling qualities and dramatic incidents of their lives, *For Better, For Worse* has received the benefit of Cecil B. DeMille's best skill. His direction has given it the tempo, distinction and perfect play of every feature required."

Edward Weitzel in
The Moving Picture World,
May 10, 1919.

Gloria Swanson, Wanda Hawley, and Elliott Dexter

Wanda Hawley, Tom Forman, and Gloria Swanson

172

"Dropping the elegant thrusts of *Don't Change Your Husband* and *Old Wives for New*, Cecil B. DeMille goes straight to the heart in *For Better, For Worse*, his latest opus. And no Cupid's dart ever found its mark with greater accuracy than does DeMille in this instance. It seems a shame to label much of the action here as 'heart stuff,' even though it is known by such a commonplace term in the production art. But certain it is that the times are almost innumerable when the skill of the director fairly makes the heart cry out."

Peter Milne in
The Motion Picture News,
May 10, 1919.

Gloria Swanson, Wanda Hawley, Elliott Dexter, and Raymond Hatton

Gloria Swanson

Theodore Roberts

174

Gloria Swanson, Lila Lee, Mildred Reardon,
and Thomas Meighan

MALE
AND FEMALE

Produced and directed by Cecil B. DeMille. Scenario by Jeanie Macpherson, founded on the play, The Admirable Crichton, *by James M. Barrie Cameraman: Alvin Wyckoff. Film Editor: Anne Bauchens. Released by Famous Players-Lasky Corp. on the Paramount Program, November 30, 1919. Nine reels.*

STORY

Lady Mary Lasenby is betrothed to Lord Brockelhurst, although neither really loves the other. In the downstairs servants' quarters the butler Crichton is adored by the scullery maid, Tweeny. Everybody goes on a sailing excursion on Lord Loam's yacht, which is wrecked, and the noble, pampered castaways find themselves on a desert island with Crichton and Tweeny. Now it is Crichton who takes over as the true noble master, showing the others how to survive on the bare essentials at hand. Lady Mary balks at being forced to do menial labor, but comes to love Crichton, and they plan to wed. The whole party is rescued, however, and they return to

175

Gloria Swanson, Thomas Meighan, and Lila Lee

Gloria Swanson and Mildred Reardon

England, where class distinction soon asserts itself, with Lady Mary wedding Lord Brockelhurst as had originally been planned, and Crichton taking Tweeny as his bride.

CAST

Lady Mary Lasenby	Gloria Swanson
Crichton, a Butler	Thomas Meighan
Tweeny	Lila Lee
Lord Loam	Theodore Roberts
Hon. Ernest Wolley	Raymond Hatton
Agatha Lasenby	Mildred Reardon
The King's Favorite	Bebe Daniels
Lord Brockelhurst	Robert Cain
Susan	Julia Faye
Lady Eileen	
Dun Craigie	Rhy Darby
Lady Brockelhurst	Maym Kelso
Treherne	Edward (Edmund) Burns
McGuire	Henry Woodward
Thomas	Sydney Deane
"Buttons"	Wesley Barry
Fisher	Edna Mae Cooper
Mrs. Perkins	Lillian Leighton
Pilot of Lord Loam's	
Yacht	Guy Oliver
Captain of Yacht	Clarence Burton

Thomas Meighan and Gloria Swanson

176

REVIEWS

"That Cecil B. DeMille has proven himself one of the foremost directors on the screen has long been recognized. It looks as if he has excelled himself with *Male and Female*, an adaptation of Sir James M. Barrie's play, *The Admirable Crichton*. There may be those who will find fault that the original title has been changed, but if they know the British playwright they will appreciate the fact that he cannot be done successfully on the screen. So *Male and Female* is Cecil B. DeMille's achievement any way you look at it. True, he has incorporated Barrie's underlying thought that English life is divided by sharp contrasts—that equality does not figure in it except in moments of extremity. And when stressful events are over, things are as they were in the beginning."

Laurence Reid in
The Motion Picture News,
December 6, 1919.

"A truly gorgeous panorama, unwound about the story contained in J. M. Barrie's play, *The Admirable Crichton*, with Miss Macpherson as the composer of the optic version, and Mr. DeMille as the conductor and expounder. It is a typical DeMille production—audacious, glittering, intriguing, superlatively elegant, and quite without heart. It reminds me of one of our great California flowers, glowing with all the colors of the rainbow and devoid of fragrance."

Julian Johnson in
Photoplay Magazine,
December, 1919.

Lila Lee, Raymond Hatton, Mildred Reardon, and Edmund Burns

Gloria Swanson

Bebe Daniels

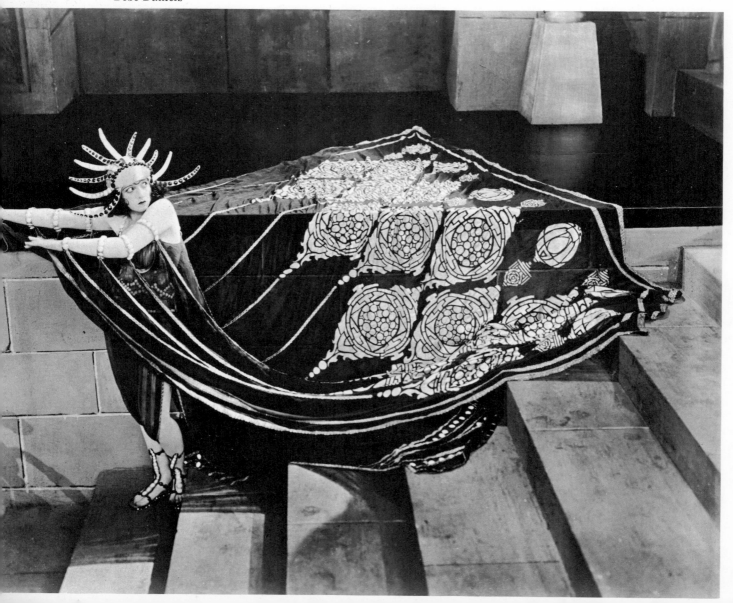

Gloria Swanson

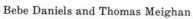
Bebe Daniels and Thomas Meighan

180

Gloria Swanson and Thomas Meighan

WHY CHANGE YOUR WIFE?

Produced and directed by Cecil B. DeMille. Scenario by Olga Printzlau and Sada Cowan, adapted from a story by William C. de Mille. Cameraman: Alvin Wyckoff. Film Editor: Anne Bauchens. Produced by Artcraft Pictures Corp., released by Famous Players-Lasky Corp. on the Paramount Program, May 2, 1920. Seven reels.

STORY

Robert Gordon and his wife Beth are completely unalike; he is a bit of a hedonist; she prosaic and intellectual. He goes out one night to a cabaret and meets Sally Clark, a girl after his own tastes, and next morning Beth, noticing the scent of perfume on his clothes, quarrels with him. They separate and are divorced. Gordon soon finds that Sally is too flashy and superficial for him, while Beth just as quickly finds that she has let herself become dowdy. She begins to look after herself, and buys a new wardrobe. Made over and now a ravishing beauty, she meets her former husband at a fashionable summer resort, and they fall in love again. But Gordon is acci-

Thomas Meighan, Gloria Swanson, and Theodore Kosloff

dentally injured, and Beth takes him to her
home, where the doctor tells her that he cannot
be moved until he is better. Sally is miffed at
first, but then is reconciled, saying, "The only
good thing about marriage, anyway, is the ali-
mony."

CAST

Beth Gordon	Gloria Swanson
Robert Gordon	Thomas Meighan
Sally Clark	Bebe Daniels
Radinoff	Theodore Kosloff
Aunt Kate	Sylvia Ashton
The Doctor	Clarence Geldart
Harriette	Maym Kelso
Butler	Lucien Littlefield
Maid	Edna Mae Cooper
A Woman Client	Jane Wolfe

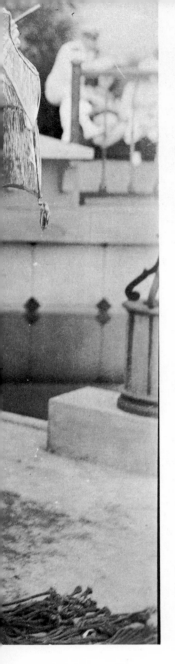

Gloria Swanson

REVIEWS

"Cecil B. DeMille has hit the bulls-eye again. *Why Change Your Wife?*, his latest Paramount release, is totally different in character from *Male and Female*. It is a comedy satire on married life. Nothing of a farcical nature is introduced. It is truth itself, with rare bits of sparkling drama, and it runs along smoothly and fast."

M. A. Malaney in
The Moving Picture World,
March 6, 1920.

"This Paramount feature by Cecil B. DeMille isn't a great feature, but it's a good market product. Lots of advertising dodges can be honestly used in connection with it to coax patronage. Papa will want Mamma to see it, and the children will get their share of enjoyment from it, but Mr. DeMille is too obvious a workman to touch the high points of the imagination. What he has done is to preach a good everyday sermon in story form."

The Weekly *Variety*,
April 30, 1920.

Thomas Meighan and Bebe Daniels

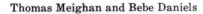

183

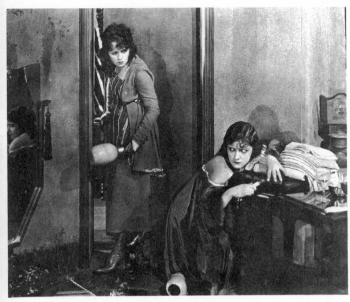

Bebe Daniels and Gloria Swanson

"Just now director DeMille is at the extra-seasoning stage. Having achieved a reputation as the great modern concocter of the sex stew by adding a piquant dash here and there to *Don't Change Your Husband*, and a little something more to *Male and Female*, he spills the spice box into *Why Change Your Wife?* and the result is a rare concoction—the most gorgeously sensual film of the month; in decoration the most costly, in physical allure the most fascinating, in effect the most immoral."

Burns Mantle in
Photoplay Magazine,
May, 1920.

Bebe Daniels and Thomas Meighan

Gloria Swanson

Mickey Moore, Elliott Dexter, and Gloria Swanson

SOMETHING TO THINK ABOUT

Produced and directed by Cecil B. DeMille. Original scenario by Jeanie Macpherson. Cameramen: Alvin Wyckoff and Karl Struss. Film Editor: Anne Bauchens. Presented by Jesse L. Lasky for Artcraft Pictures Corp., released by Famous Players-Lasky Corp. on the Paramount Program, October 24, 1920. Seven reels.

STORY

David Markley, a wealthy cripple living in a small town, finances the education of the blacksmith's daughter, Ruth Anderson. When she returns to her hometown, Markley falls in love with her and asks her to marry him. She consents out of gratitude, but then elopes with a city worker, Jim Dirk, and marries him. Dirk is killed in a subway accident, and Ruth returns to the small town, where she is renounced by her now-blind father. Markley marries her in name

187

only to benefit the son she has borne Dirk—but Ruth and Markley fall in love, and her love for him drives away his bitterness and makes him physically whole once again.

CAST

David Markley	Elliott Dexter
Ruth Anderson	Gloria Swanson
Jim Dirk	Monte Blue
Luke Anderson	Theodore Roberts
Housekeeper	Claire McDowell
Bobby	Mickey Moore
The Banker's Daughter	Julia Faye
A Country Masher	James Mason
A Servant	Togo Yammamoto
A Clown	Theodore Kosloff

REVIEWS

"It is a different DeMille who comes forward with *Something to Think About*. The DeMille of *Why Change Your Wife?* has taken upon himself the burden of giving expression to the spiritual drama, thus stopping the critics who took him to task for reveling in sex. And this distinctly different picture offers anew the impression that whatever he touches is done well. The offering has truly moving moments despite a melodramatic flair which destroys its simplicity to a degree. But DeMille is such a master workman and offers such skill at situation and climax that the spectator is keenly interested."

Laurence Reid in
The Motion Picture News,
October 30, 1920.

"The title is an invitation to meditate upon the moral of the story rather than a name growing out of and descriptive of the tale itself. Just what the moral is does not appear very plainly. Perhaps the writer and producer sought to teach the lesson of *The Miracle Man* that faith accomplishes all things. Several passages at the close of the film play would seem to indicate some such purpose, but the whole thing is confused and foggy as to intent."

The Weekly *Variety*,
October 22, 1920.

Theodore Roberts and Gloria Swanson

Gloria Swanson and Elliott Dexter

Forrest Stanley and Agnes Ayres

190

FORBIDDEN FRUIT

Produced and directed by Cecil B. DeMille. Scenario by Jeanie Macpherson, based upon The Golden Chance, *an original scenario written by her and DeMille, and produced in 1915. Cameraman: Alvin Wyckoff. Film Editor: Anne Bauchens. Released by the Famous Players-Lasky Corp. on the Paramount Program, February 12, 1921. Eight reels.*

STORY

The characters' names are altered, and DeMille added an elaborate flashback of the *Cinderella* story; otherwise, the story remains substantially the same as that of *The Golden Chance*, which DeMille directed in 1915.

Agnes Ayres and Kathlyn Williams

CAST

Mary Maddock	Agnes Ayres
Steve Maddock	Clarence Burton
James Harrington Mallory	Theodore Roberts
Mrs. Mallory	Kathlyn Williams
Nelson Rogers	Forrest Stanley
Pietro Guiseppe	Theodore Kosloff
Nadia Craig	Shannon Day
John Craig	Bertram Johns
Maid	Julia Faye

REVIEWS

"*Forbidden Fruit*, above everything else, has been lavishly produced. A great many precious shekels have been spent to make this feature one that will not only make a dramatic appeal, but will dazzle everyone who sees it by the gorgeous settings that are inducted into the story in phantasmagoria form."

The Dramatic Mirror and Theatre World, February 21, 1921.

"*Forbidden Fruit* is melodrama, and in less artistic hands could have been made a painful joke. But DeMille brings out with characteristic deftness every value put into the play by Jeanie Macpherson, and the result is a well told, smooth-running, and skilfully developed romance.... In addition to telling his story superbly, DeMille has interpolated, as a sort of pictorial obligato, the story of Cinderella in a fashion probably never attained before. The photography here and all through the picture is flawless, the lightings exquisite."

The Weekly *Variety*, January 28, 1921.

Clarence Burton, Agnes Ayres, and Kathlyn Williams

Agnes Ayres and Kathlyn Williams

Forrest Stanley and Agnes Ayres

Wanda Hawley

Wallace Reid

Wanda Hawley

THE AFFAIRS OF ANATOL

Produced and directed by Cecil B. DeMille. Scenario by Jeanie Macpherson, Beulah Marie Dix, Lorna Moon and Elmer Harris, suggested by Arthur Schnitzler's play Anatol *and the paraphrase thereof by Granville Barker. Cameramen: Alvin Wyckoff and Karl Struss. Film Editor: Anne Bauchens. Released by Famous Players-Lasky Corp. as a DeMille-Paramount Special, September 18, 1921. Nine reels.*

STORY

Anatol DeWitt Spencer, Park Avenue socialite, confesses to his friend Max Runyon that there is too much "honey" in his honeymoon; he finds fault with Vivian, his bride, and goes looking for romance, first with Emilie, a blonde he had known in his youth. He sets up Emilie, now a cabaret girl and gold-digger, in an expensive apartment, but when he finds that she is two-timing him with a rich old wolf, Gordon Bron-son, he wrecks her apartment, and returns to his wife. They go to the country on a second honeymoon, he still secretly seeking the ideal female companionship. In the countryside he encounters Annie Elliott, who has tried to drown herself because a misunderstanding husband drove her to rob him of charity funds in order to buy some dainty lingerie. Annie also proves to have her flaws, however, for she robs Anatol of his wallet in order to replace the money she has stolen. Thoroughly disillusioned with women who represent themselves as good, Anatol turns to Satan Synne, known as "the wickedest woman in New York," only to find that the notorious "Satan" is really virtuous Mary Deacon, willing to do anything in order to gain money to aid her husband, who is in the hospital facing expensive surgery. Deciding to bear with the evils he has, Anatol gratefully returns to Vivian, discovering that he is jealous of her because in his absence she is socializing with his best friend Max. "Truth is dead," cries a weary Anatol. "Long live illusion."

CAST

Anatol DeWitt Spencer	Wallace Reid
Vivian, his wife	Gloria Swanson
Max Runyon	Elliott Dexter
Satan Synne	Bebe Daniels
Abner Elliott	Monte Blue
Emilie Dixon	Wanda Hawley
Gordon Bronson	Theodore Roberts
Annie Elliott	Agnes Ayres
Nazzer Singh	Theodore Kosloff
Orchestra Leader	Polly Moran
Hoffmeier	Raymond Hatton
Tibra	Julia Faye
Dr. Bowles	Charles Ogle
Dr. Johnson	Winter Hall
The Spencer Butler	Guy Oliver
The Spencer Maid	Ruth Miller
The Spencer Valet	Lucien Littlefield
Nurse	Zelma Maja
Chorus Girl	Shannon Day
Bridge Players	Elinor Glyn
	Lady Parker

Bebe Daniels

Bebe Daniels, Agnes Ayres, Gloria Swanson, DeMille, and Wanda Hawley

Raymond Hatton, Elliott Dexter, DeMille, Theodore Roberts, Wallace Reid, Monte Blue and Theodore Kosloff

Ruth Miller and Wallace Reid

Guests	William Boyd
	Maud Wayne
Stage Manager	Fred Huntley
Chorus Girl	Alma Bennett

REVIEWS

"As a box-office magnet the picture can not fail. It will please audiences from a dozen different angles and it has quite as many exploitation possibilities. If ever a picture was sure-fire, for big cities and little towns alike, this is one. The man who doesn't sell out for every performance of a double run should turn his show shop into a Quaker meeting house."

J. S. Dickerson in
The Motion Picture News,
September 24, 1921.

"Should be enormously popular, especially with those who think Schnitzler is a cheese."

Robert E. Sherwood in
Life,
September 18, 1921.

"If a huge sum was given for the screen rights to Schnitzler's *The Affairs of Anatol* in order that the new Cecil B. DeMille production might be, it is a glaring example of extravagance. With the characters called by other names and the main title *Five Kisses*, as was, for a time, intended, there would have been no infringement. Certainly this *deluxe* review of ladies fair, boudoirs and cabarets is a far-fetched version of the sophisticated Viennese tale."

Adele Whitely Fletcher in
The Motion Picture Magazine,
September, 1921.

197

Wallace Reid and Gloria Swanson

"Cecil DeMille, not Arthur Schnitzler. We leave it to you which gentleman has pleased our public more . . . . Good entertainment, but not for the children."

Photoplay Magazine,
September, 1921.

Wallace Reid and
Bebe Daniels

Theodore Roberts

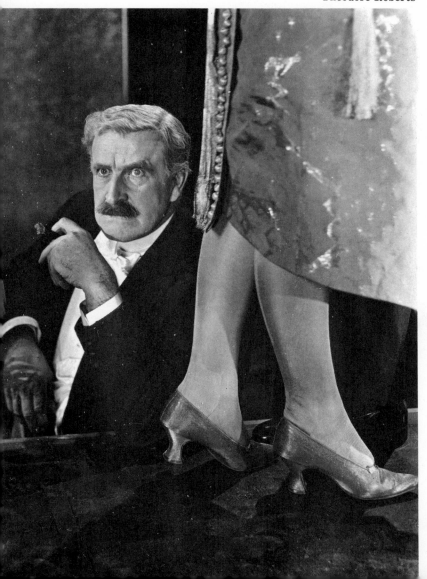

199

Conrad Nagel (*in white suit*)

Conrad Nagel and Mildred Harris

FOOL'S PARADISE

Produced and directed by Cecil B. DeMille. Scenario by Beulah Marie Dix and Sada Cowan, suggested by the short story, "The Laurels and the Lady," by Leonard Merrick. Cameraman: Alvin Wyckoff. Film Editor: Anne Bauchens. Presented by Jesse L. Lasky for release by Famous Players-Lasky Corp. on the Paramount Program, December 9, 1921. Nine reels.

STORY

Arthur Phelps, a war veteran, befriends a cantina girl, Poll Patchouli, one night in a Mexican border oil town. She falls in love with him, and is jealous when she sees that he is carrying a torch for Rosa Duchene, a dancer. Poll, as a joke, gives a trick cigar to Phelps, and when the flash goes off, he is blinded. His friendship for Poll turns to hatred. But she impersonates Rosa, and he believes that at last he has gained Rosa's love, that she has come to him in his need. Phelps and Poll marry, and she arranges for surgery for his eyes. The surgery is successful, and when Phelps sees how he has been duped, he leaves Poll to chase halfway around the world to Siam

201

Conrad Nagel and Joan Davidson

Dorothy Dalton and Theodore Kosloff

in search of Rosa, only to learn dramatically of her true selfishness and heartlessness. He returns to seek out Poll; she saves his life almost at the cost of her own, and they realize their mutual love.

CAST

Poll Patchouli	Dorothy Dalton
Arthur Phelps	Conrad Nagel
Rosa Duchene	Mildred Harris
John Roderiguez	Theodore Kosloff
Prince Talaat-Ni	John Davidson
Samaran, his Chief Wife	Julia Faye
Manuel	Clarence Burton
Briggs	Guy Oliver
Girda	Jacqueline Logan
Kay	Kamuela Searle

REVIEWS

"Jesse Lasky presented the Cecil B. DeMille production, *Fool's Paradise*, at the Criterion, December 9, as a 'special'; it is that in every sense of the word. As a production, it speaks of unlimited expenditure in the making; as an entertainment, it is wonderfully satisfying, and it should stand up with anything that DeMille has done heretofore as a box-office attraction."

The Weekly *Variety*,
December 16, 1921.

"Cecil B. DeMille will either put over a Barnum and Bailey show in his screen documents or pull down the tent and rent out the land for pasture. The director, highly imaginative and ever keen

Mildred Harris,
Kamuela Searle,
and Jacqueline Logan

Dorothy Dalton
and Conrad Nagel

John Davidson, Mildred Harris, and Conrad Nagel

to bewilder the eye with dazzling scenes, has concocted a fascinating picture in *Fool's Paradise*, in spite of the fact that his story goes astray while he puts on an after-show."

Laurence Reid in
The Motion Picture News,
December 24, 1921.

Dorothy Dalton

Dorothy Dalton

Mildred Harris and Jacqueline Logan

Theodore Roberts, Jack Mower,
and Leatrice Joy

Leatrice Joy

Edith Roberts

Winter Hall, Edith Roberts, and John Davidson

SATURDAY NIGHT

Produced and directed by Cecil B. DeMille. Original scenario by Jeanie Macpherson. Cameraman: Alvin Wyckoff. Film Editor: Anne Bauchens. Released by Famous Players-Lasky Corp. on the Paramount Program, January 29, 1922. Nine reels.

STORY

A society butterfly, Iris Van Suydam, is betrothed to Richard Prentiss, a man of her own class; but one day when the family's handsome chauffeur, Tom McGuire, is out with Iris in the limousine, he saves her life when the car is trapped on a railroad trestle in the path of an approaching train. Iris falls in love with and marries McGuire. Prentiss similarly is attracted to the family laundress' daughter, Shamrock

O'Day, and weds her. But neither marriage works out, as neither of the upper-class characters can adjust to the established ways of life of their mates, and vice-versa. Iris is trapped in a tenement fire, from which she is rescued by Prentiss. Two divorces and two new marriages later, the couples are properly mated—Iris with Prentiss and Shamrock with McGuire.

CAST

Iris Van Suydam	Leatrice Joy
Richard Prentiss	Conrad Nagel
Shamrock O'Day	Edith Roberts
Tom McGuire	Jack Mower
Elsie Prentiss	Julia Faye
Mrs. Prentiss	Edythe Chapman
Uncle	Theodore Roberts
Mrs. O'Day	Sylvia Ashton
The Count	John Davidson
Tompkins	James Neill
The Professor	Winter Hall

Leatrice Joy

Leatrice Joy

Edith Roberts and Conrad Nagel

Leatrice Joy and Conrad Nagel

REVIEWS

"*Saturday Night* is rather a peculiar offering for a DeMille picture. The first three or four reels are typical, relating through original and entertaining incident, titles, etc., what happened to bring about the marriage of a society bud to her chauffeur and of a rich young businessman, fiancé of the girl referred to, to the daughter of his laundress. Then comes a series of sequences, rather on the farce comedy order, in which the 'oil and water will not mix' idea is gotten over. Following this is some melodrama—a very well done fire scene with the heroine rescued in a realistic manner."

J. S. Dickerson in
The Motion Picture News,
February 4, 1922.

"There's no doubt the picture can take its place as a box-office feature, for DeMille's name and the lavishness with which he has done the home life of the 'ritz' characters, though somewhat reflective of former palatial residences as conceived by him, will satisfy. Also, the pictorial narrative of romance connected with the interclass marriage idea will always appeal strongly to the majority of the fair sex."

The Weekly *Variety*,
January 27, 1922.

"We really do not understand why Mr. DeMille wastes his talents as a motion picture director. There are lots of directors, and some of them we understand are out of employment. But when it comes to the creation of a bizarre bed or a fantastic negligee or a rococo bathroom, no one can touch Mr. DeMille, not even the police, apparently. Why some bathroom fixtures company or some specialty shop which wants to build up an enormous trade among the nouveau-riche has not engaged him as Extraordinary Advisor is beyond our small comprehension."

Arthur Denison in
The Filmplay Journal,
April, 1922.

Leatrice Joy

Leatrice Joy,
Thomas Meighan,
Lois Wilson, and players

Leatrice Joy, Thomas Meighan, Casson Ferguson,
John Miltern, and players

MANSLAUGHTER

Produced and directed by Cecil B. DeMille. Scenario by Jeanie Macpherson, adapted from the novel by Alice Duer Miller. Cameraman: Alvin Wyckoff. Film Editor: Anne Bauchens. Presented by Jesse L. Lasky as a Famous Players-Lasky Corp. release on the Paramount Pictures Program, September 24, 1922. Ten reels.

STORY

Lydia Thorne, a wealthy society girl, craves excitement, and in racing a motorcycle policeman trying to arrest her, she is responsible for his death. Arrested and brought to trial for manslaughter, she is prosecuted by the district attorney, Daniel O'Bannon, her fiancé. O'Bannon realizes her only hope of salvation is conviction and serving a prison sentence. He paints a lurid, dramatic picture of the downfall of Rome by its sensation seekers, and Lydia, convicted, is sent to prison. This breaks O'Bannon's moral fiber, and he becomes an alcoholic. In prison, Lydia sees the error of her ways, and reforms. When she is released, she seeks out O'Bannon, and her own regeneration inspires him to finding himself. Together, they face a new life.

Thomas Meighan and Leatrice Joy

John Miltern, Thomas Meighan, and Leatrice Joy

REVIEWS

"Looking aside for the moment from the spectacular side of this newest DeMille achievement—its reproduction of decadent Rome under the Caesars, its lavishness displayed in the cabaret sets, and the opulence suggestive of the manner in which the idle rich live—looking aside from all these typically DeMille effects, we must give him credit for building the most direct action which has graced the screen in many a day. It is direct story-telling, think what you may of the theatrical character of the plot. It moves and by moving holds your attention through a chain of events dramatic, perhaps impossible, but which points a moral notwithstanding."

Laurence Reid in
The Motion Picture News,
September 30, 1922.

"Cecil B. DeMille's direction carried several trademarks allowing for the DeMille mob ensembles in a Caesarian touch, showing the debauch of the ancient as compared to a modern version in a smart roadhouse. This set ran into money; in fact, the entire production looked lavish."

The Weekly *Variety*,
September 22, 1922.

Leatrice Joy and Thomas Meighan

Leatrice Joy

Lois Wilson and Leatrice Joy

George Fawcett and Lois Wilson

The Roman orgy

Anna Q. Nilsson and Theodore Kosloff

Milton Sills,
Pauline Garon,
and Theodore Kosloff

Anna Q. Nilsson and Theodore Kosloff

ADAM'S RIB

Produced and directed by Cecil B. DeMille. Original scenario by Jeanie Macpherson. Cameraman: Alvin Wyckoff. Film Editor: Anne Bauchens. Presented by Jesse L. Lasky for release by Famous Players-Lasky Corp. on the Paramount Pictures Corp. Program, March 4, 1923. Ten reels.

STORY

Middle-aged and social-minded Mrs. Michael Ramsay, finding herself left to her own resources by a husband whose only interest is in amassing a fortune in wheat, is attracted by a nobleman and plans to elope with him. Her flapper daughter, Mathilda, determined to prevent a scandal, follows her mother, who is caught in a compromising situation, for which the daughter assumes guilt, and her fiancé marries her to protect her good name. Ramsay nearly goes broke on the wheat market, but when he saves himself and makes a new fortune, his contrite wife returns to his bed and board, and he forgives her.

CAST

Michael Ramsay	Milton Sills
Prof. Nathan Reade	Elliott Dexter
M. Jaromir, King of Moravia	Theodore Kosloff
Mrs. Michael Ramsay	Anna Q. Nilsson
Mathilda Ramsay	Pauline Garon
"The Mischievous One"	Julia Faye
James Kilkenna	Clarence Geldart
Minister to Moravia	George Field
Hugo Kermaier	Robert Brower
Kramer	Forrest Robinson
Lieut. Braschek	Gino Corrado
Secretary to Minister	Wedgewood Nowell
Cave Man	Clarence Burton

REVIEWS

The ornate DeMille's latest—and worst. Apparently DeMille started out to do an epic of the flapper. Yet this is just the old tale of the girl who sacrifices her reputation to save another woman, this time her flirtative mother..... This seems to mark the complete collapse of the man who could once intrigue audiences with his daring, howbeit garish, boudoir revelations. *Adam's Rib* is a mass of utter absurdities with a good box-office title."

> Frederick James Smith in
> *Photoplay Magazine*,
> May, 1923.

"A silly, piffling screenplay, dealing with husband and wife sex subject in a peculiarly crude and obvious style, but a picture that probably is destined to make a lot of money . . . . It looks like another case of *The Sheik*, only this story is even more foolish."

> The Weekly *Variety*,
> March 1, 1923.

"*Adam's Rib* is somewhat above the usual DeMille standard—which statement may be added to the Dictionary of Faint Praise."

> Robert E. Sherwood in
> *Life*,
> March 29, 1923.

Milton Sills, Pauline Garon,
and Anna Q. Nilsson

Pauline Garon, Elliott Dexter,
and Milton Sills

216

Milton Sills
and Anna Q. Nilsson

DeMille and Pauline Garon

Pauline Garon and Elliott Dexter

217

Pauline Garon and Elliott Dexter

Milton Sills

218

Anna Q. Nilsson and Milton Sills

219

Theodore Roberts

THE TEN COMMANDMENTS

Produced and directed by Cecil B. DeMille. Scenario by Jeanie Macpherson, adapted from the Book of Exodus and a modern story by Miss Macpherson. Cameramen: Bert Glennon, assisted by Edward S. Curtis, J. Peverell Marley, Fred Westerberg, Archibald J. Stout, Donald Biddle Keyes. Color Photography: Ray Rennahan. Film Editor: Anne Bauchens. Presented by Adolph Zukor and Jesse L. Lasky for release by Famous Players-Lasky Corp. on the Paramount Pictures Program, as a special DeMille Production, November 23, 1923. Fourteen reels.

STORY

The first part, in Technicolor, deals with the biblical tale of Moses leading the Children of Israel from bondage under the Egyptian pharaohs out into the Promised Land. They forsake their God to worship the Golden Calf when Moses goes to the top of Mount Sinai to receive the Ten Commandments written by the hand of God on tablets of stone. When Moses comes down from the mountain to see what his people have done, he rejects them by casting the Commandments aside.

The second part, in black and white, is a sermon dealing with a story of today, showing the efficacy of the Ten Commandments in modern life. Two brothers in San Francisco, John and Dan McTavish, love the same girl, Mary Leigh, a waif brought into their home to be cared for by their Bible-reverencing mother. Mary is infatuated by the younger brother, Dan, and marries him. Dan, in association with a crooked politician, Redding, rises fast in the contracting world, and is guilty of graft in constructing a big new cathedral, using one part of cement to twelve parts of sand. John, who has been made carpentry foreman, discovers his brother's crime, but too late, for the brothers' mother has wandered into the cathedral and is killed when the whole apse wall crumbles and buries her in the ruins. Dan and Mary have drifted apart, and Dan has taken a Eurasian mistress, Sally Lung, from whom he contracts leprosy. He kills Sally, and tries to flee to Mexico in his motorboat, the "Defiance," but a storm comes up, and he is killed when the boat is dashed to pieces upon a rock. Mary, believing she too has contracted leprosy, attempts suicide, but is saved by John, and she learns that through prayer and faith she can regain purity.

CAST

Part I:

Moses, the Lawgiver	Theodore Roberts
Rameses, the Magnificent	Charles de Roche
Miriam, Sister of Moses	Estelle Taylor
The Wife of Pharaoh	Julia Faye
The Son of Pharaoh	Terrence Moore
Aaron, Brother of Moses	James Neill
Dathan, the Discontented	Lawson Butt
The Taskmaster	Clarence Burton
The Bronze Man	Noble Johnson

Part II:

Mrs. Martha McTavish	Edythe Chapman
John McTavish	Richard Dix
Dan McTavish	Rod La Rocque
Mary Leigh	Leatrice Joy
Sally Lung	Nita Naldi
Redding, an Inspector	Robert Edeson
The Doctor	Charles Ogle
The Outcast	Agnes Ayres

Rod LaRocque and Nita Naldi

REVIEWS

"Mr. DeMille, in his time, has motivated the works of many writers—from James Matthew Barrie to Alice Duer Miller—has sacrificed their ideas to make a Hollywood holiday. But when, in *The Ten Commandments,* he approached the words of God, he became suddenly overwhelmed with the idea that it would be better to set them forth unchanged. In this, Mr. DeMille displayed commendable originality; for no literary work has had rougher treatment from the public at large. If the mighty Cecil had seen fit to step on the Ten Commandments, he would at least have had plenty of precedent for the act."

Robert E. Sherwood in
Life,
January 17, 1924.

"The best photoplay ever made. The greatest theatrical spectacle in history. The greatest sermon on the tablets which form the basis of all law ever preached. Strong words, indeed, but written two weeks after seeing it, after serious consideration of Griffith's *Intolerance* and *Birth of a Nation.* It will last as long as the film on which it is recorded. It wipes the slate clean of charges of an immoral influence against the screen."

James R. Quirk in
Photoplay Magazine,
February, 1924.

224

Leatrice Joy and Rod LaRocque

Leatrice Joy and Richard Dix

Rod LaRocque and Richard Dix

Nita Naldi

Theodore Roberts

Rod LaRocque and Nita Naldi

Estelle Taylor in the Golden Calf scene

Charles DeRoche

Estelle Taylor

Rod LaRocque and Robert Edeson

230

Rod LaRocque and George Fawcett

TRIUMPH

Produced and directed by Cecil B. DeMille. Scenario by Jeanie Macpherson, adapted from the novel by May Edington. Cameraman: J. Peverell Marley. Film Editor: Anne Bauchens. Music compiled by James C. Bradford. Presented by Adolph Zukor and Jesse L. Lasky, for release by the Famous Players-Lasky Corp. on the Paramount Pictures Program, April 27, 1924. Eight reels.

STORY

When a tin magnate dies, he leaves a will stating that if his spendthrift son, King Garnet, doesn't settle down within two years, the source of the family income shall pass into the hands of another son by a secret marriage, William Silver, who is the manager of the tin factory. Garnet continues to whoop it up, however, and at the end of two years is a bum on a park bench, while Silver has assumed leadership of the factory.

Both men have been in love with the factory's forewoman, Ann Land, who has operatic aspirations. Silver encourages her; she studies and has success abroad, but smoke from a theatre fire ruins her voice forever. The factory faces a labor crisis, and Garnet, now a factory employe, aids Silver and Ann in putting everything in order. The three work in close harmony, and Garnet weds Ann.

Rod LaRocque and Leatrice Joy

Victor Varconi, Theodore Kosloff, and Leatrice Joy

CAST

Ann Land	Leatrice Joy
King Garnet	Rod La Rocque
William Silver	Victor Varconi
James Martin	Charles Ogle
Varinoff	Theodore Kosloff
Samuel Overton	Robert Edeson
Countess Rika	Julia Faye
David Garnet	George Fawcett
Torrini	Spottiswoode Aitken
A Factory Girl	ZaSu Pitts
A Tramp	Raymond Hatton
The Flower Girl	Alma Bennett
A Painter	Jimmie Adams

REVIEWS

"*Triumph* is a surprise in more ways than one. It lacks the terrific ostentation, the bizarre blather of *Male and Female, Fool's Paradise,* and the rest. Indeed it seems that a miracle has come to pass: Cecil B. DeMille has lost his fondness for putting on the dog. All this is particularly pleasing to your correspondent. I have always wanted to be pals with Mr. DeMille, but it has been difficult for me to accomplish this end—chiefly because he and I have had such radically different ideas about plumbing. From his treatment of *Triumph* it would seem that hereafter he intends to picture bathrooms that look like bathrooms, social functions that look like social functions, and characters that act like human beings.

Charles Ogle, Leatrice Joy, Victor Varconi,
Robert Edeson, and ZaSu Pitts

Rod LaRocque, Leatrice Joy, and Victor Varconi

Leatrice Joy, Rod LaRocque, and Victor Varconi

(*In center*) ZaSu Pitts

So everybody's happy, and I can now devote my entire attention to Rupert Hughes."

Robert E. Sherwood in
Life,
May 22, 1924.

"Two minutes shy of an hour and a half in running time, the feature could undoubtedly assume deletion without a harmful effect, although DeMille has so routined the continuity that the story never becomes an out-and-out burden."

The Weekly *Variety,*
April 23, 1924.

"Success in 'super spectacle' realms of photoplay production has not spoiled Mr. Cecil B. DeMille for the more formal type of featurelength picture. *Triumph* is his first effort since *The Ten Commandments,* and it is here rather confidently stated that rarely if ever is more satisfactory, well-rounded entertainment to be production. . . . There is plenty of glitter to the production. . . . Mr. DeMille has included a costume sequence. It is short but very dressy and shows a flash of Romeo chanting his song of love to Juliet on the balcony."

Thomas C. Kennedy in
The Motion Picture News,
May 3, 1924.

Vera Reynolds

Rod LaRocque, Vera Reynolds,
Robert Edeson, Julia Faye,
and Ricardo Cortez

Julia Faye and Ricardo Cortez

FEET OF CLAY

Produced and directed by Cecil B. DeMille. Scenario by Beulah Marie Dix and Bertram Milhauser, adapted from the novel by Margaretta Tuttle. Cameramen: J. Peverell Marley and Archibald J. Stout. Film Editor: Anne Bauchens. Presented by Adolph Zukor and Jesse L. Lasky for release by the Famous Players-Lasky Corp. on the Paramount Pictures Program, September 28, 1924. Ten reels.

STORY

Well-born but poor, Kerry Harlan moves in top society, and falls in love with Amy Loring, stepsister to Bertha Lansell, wife of a prominent surgeon. Kerry saves Amy's life in a surfboard race off the coast of Catalina at the price of being bitten on the foot by a killer shark. Dr. Lansell warns Kerry he must stay off his feet for a year. Amy and Kerry marry, and she supports them by working as a fashion model. But Bertha Lansell is infatuated with Kerry, and does everything to win him as her lover. Her doctor-husband suspects her, and follows her to the Harlan apartment, and Bertha, hiding on a narrow ledge outside the window, accidentally falls to her death. A scandal ensues, and Amy and Kerry make a suicide pact to die together by gas; but their souls are returned to earth when their bodies are discovered and brought back to life.

Ricardo Cortez, Vera Reynolds, and Rod LaRocque

Ricardo Cortez, Julia Faye, Rod LaRocque,
Robert Edeson, Vera Reynolds, and William Boyd

Vera Reynolds and Rod LaRocque *(in the Afterworld)*

236

Vera Reynolds and Rod LaRocque

CAST

Amy Loring	Vera Reynolds
Kerry Harlan	Rod La Rocque
Bertha Lansell	Julia Faye
Tony Channing	Ricardo Cortez
Dr. Fergus Lansell	Robert Edeson
Bendick	Theodore Kosloff
The Bookkeeper	Victor Varconi
Young Society Man	William Boyd

REVIEWS

"This is a typical Cecil B. DeMille picture. We have come to expect something different from this showman-director and he has not failed to work in surprising novelties in this instance. Here is a combination of about all the ingredients used in modern film production. There is, first of all, the usual DeMille lavishness in scenic investiture; then there are feminine costumes that scintillate in their gorgeousness, beautiful girls, striking lighting effects, and masterful photography. Next there is a story, which, by the way, has been read by millions either in the *Ladies' Home Journal* or in novel form, and which Mr. DeMille has changed somewhat to strengthen as a picture tale. The plot packs a good moral and swings the observer along through moments of the wildest jazz, the strongest drama, real heart appeal, and passionate love-making."

Frank Elliott in
The Motion Picture News,
September 27, 1924.

"A whale of an audience picture that will tap money anywhere. It has a couple of thrills that are real thrills, and with it a society atmosphere with a full portion of sex stuff that will get over in great shape. Incidentally, Cecil DeMille hasn't a bathtub in this one, but has a wonderful jazz band dance scene that should be looked at by all of the big band leaders to catch the idea of the novelty.... It is certain to get record box-office returns, although it does seem that *Lost Souls* might have been a better title than *Feet of Clay*.

The Weekly *Variety,*
September 24, 1924.

237

Theodore Kosloff, Lillian Rich, and Robert Cain

THE GOLDEN BED

Produced and directed by Cecil B. DeMille. Scenario by Jeanie Macpherson, based on the novel first published as Tomorrow's Bread *by Wallace Irwin. Cameraman: J. Peverell Marley. Film Editor: Anne Bauchens. Presented by Adolph Zukor and Jesse L. Lasky for release by the Famous Players-Lasky Corp. on the Paramount Pictures Program, January 25, 1925. Nine reels.*

STORY

Flora Lee Peake is a selfish Southern femme fatale, who marries a rich titled European in order to save the family plantation. But Flora acquires a string of admirers on the continent. Her husband battles with one of the most ardent, and both men fall to their deaths in an icy glacier. Flora returns to the Southern mansion, and fastens her vamp claws on the young president of a rising candy concern, Admah Holtz. Flora's sister, Margaret, had helped Holtz in his rise to success, and is in love with him, but is forced to relinquish him when Flora becomes his wife. Flora's extravagances ruin Holtz, and he is sent to prison for five years for misappropriation of the company's funds. Flora then goes the downward path, and returns to die in the golden bed of the decaying plantation house, while Holtz and Margaret begin a new life together.

239

Lillian Rich

Henry B. Walthall and Vera Reynolds

CAST

Flora Lee Peake	Lillian Rich
Colonel Peake	Henry B. Walthall
Margaret Peake	Vera Reynolds
Marquis de San Pilar	Theodore Kosloff
Admah Holtz	Rod La Rocque
Bunny O'Neill	Warner Baxter
Savarac	Robert Cain
Amos Thompson	Robert Edeson
Mrs. Amos Thompson	Julia Faye
Treasurer	Charles Clary

REVIEWS

"Right in DeMille's corner, this bed thing, and for 88 minutes the reclining contrivance is anything but a fourposter. It's a story that has provided ample leeway for DeMille to indulge himself in his customary and ponderous interiors, although the script fails to carry weight, while only one player predominates, Rod La Rocque. The bed Mr. DeMille has fashioned looks more like one of those contraptions that used to arise from the Hippodrome tank. Other than that, he has a wedding to stage and a gala social event in

Lillian Rich and Warner Baxter

240

the way of a 'candy ball' that is probably as lavish as anything of its kind ever screened. To that end the picture looks money. There can be no question on that point."

The Weekly *Variety*,
January 21, 1925.

"The picture is filled with characteristic DeMille touches. The Candy Ball is unquestionably the most gorgeous and elaborate sequence of its kind ever placed on the screen. It is the 'piece de resistance' of the film. Everything is done in candy effect, even the members of the orchestra are dressed like 'lemon sticks.' Mammoth candy boxes are used as background, with luxurious pillows in candy shapes filling them. The costuming in this setting is colorful."

Frank Elliott in
The Motion Picture News,
January 31, 1925.

"Cecil B. DeMille's last and perhaps worst picture under his contract with this producing company. A lavishly stupid spectacle. A pearl onion in a platinum setting."

Photoplay Magazine,
March, 1925.

Rod LaRocque and Vera Reynolds

Warner Baxter, Lillian Rich, and two extras

241

Joseph Schildkraut and Jetta Goudal

Vera Reynolds, Joseph Schildkraut, and William Boyd

THE ROAD TO YESTERDAY

Produced and directed by Cecil B. DeMille. Scenario by Jeanie Macpherson and Beulah Marie Dix, from the play by Beulah Marie Dix and Evelyn Greenleaf Sutherland. Cameraman: J. Peverell Marley. Film Editor: Anne Bauchens. Released by Producers Distributing Corp., November 15, 1925. Ten reels.

STORY

Kenneth Paulton is in love with his beautiful wife, Malena, but she feels a curious aversion towards him, and he accuses her of being frigid. Actually, she senses that in some previous incarnation her husband has done her a great harm. Their marriage is on the brink of disaster. The romance of Jack Moreland and flapper Beth Tyrell is also headed for the shoals. All are passengers aboard an express train speeding across the American plains when there is a terrible train wreck. While unconscious, their minds revert back to a time in England when all four lives were closely involved. Paulton was then a knight and Malena a fiery gypsy. The story comes to a climax when the gypsy girl is about to be burnt at the stake. There is then a fade-back into the modern sequence when the contemporary characters, regaining consciousness, realize their chance to right the wrongs once done.

243

Joseph Schildkraut and Jetta Goudal

CAST

Kenneth Paulton	Joseph Schildkraut
Malena Paulton	Jetta Goudal
Jack Moreland	William Boyd
Beth Tyrell	Vera Reynolds
Harriet Tyrell	Trixie Friganza
Adrian Tompkyns	Casson Ferguson
Dolly Foules	Julia Faye
Hugh Armstrong	Clarence Burton
Watt Earnshaw	Charles West
Anne Vener	Josephine Norman

REVIEWS

"This is Cecil DeMille's first personally directed release through his new alliance with Producers' Distributing, although two other films made by the DeMille unit have preceded *Road to Yesterday*. Of his own special it may be said that it qualifies as first-run stuff, lavishly made, furnished with beautiful backgrounds and setting, and cast competently in every spot. To top off the generally pleasing tone of the film, DeMille has provided the greatest train wreck scene ever shot."

The Weekly *Variety*,
December 2, 1925.

"In his picturization of *The Road to Yesterday* Cecil B. DeMille adheres tenaciously to his queer flamboyant style. This new feature, his first since he stepped out of Famous Players-Lasky Corporation, not only gives him an opportunity to dilate on things in the present age, but also lends itself to more or less colorful conceptions of the Elizabethan era.... This director, whose fecund strokes have molded an enviable fortune for him, also has the chance of contrasting a great modern express train with the ramshackle conveyances of yore. All this is very well done, but through the length of the film and the observance of film work in lieu of a narrative, the chapters do not hitch up properly, and consequently the story lacks necessary clarity."

Mordaunt Hall in
The New York Times,
December 1, 1925.

Vera Reynolds and William Boyd

244

Joseph Schildkraut, Jetta Goudal, and DeMille

Vera Reynolds and Casson Ferguson

(*In center*) Victor Varconi, Elinor Fair, and William Boyd

THE VOLGA BOATMAN

Produced and directed by Cecil B. DeMille. Scenario by Lenore J. Coffee, adapted from the novel by Konrad Bercovici. Cameraman: J. Peverell Marley. Film Editor: Anne Bauchens. Released by Producers Distributing Corp., May 23, 1926. Eleven reels.

STORY

The Princess Vera of Russia, betrothed to Prince Dimitri, is attracted by the virility of Feodor, a peasant Volga boatman. The Revolution comes, and Feodor, a leader of importance, ransacks the home of the Princess Vera, demanding either her life or that of her father when a palace servant kills one of his followers. The Princess demands that she be the one to be sacrificed, but Feodor has fallen in love with her, and fakes her death. When the ruse is discovered, he escapes with the Princess to an inn between the opposing armies, where Feodor introduces her to the other revolutionists as his wife. The royalist army invades, and the Princess is subjected to great indignities until she is recognized by the Prince Dimitri and saved. Feodor is ordered shot, but the Princess saves him. The revolutionists regain power, and Dimitri is allowed to go into exile, while the Princess joins Feodor and returns to Russia with him.

CAST

Feodor, a Volga Boatman	William Boyd
Verna, a Princess	Elinor Fair
Prince Nikita, her Father	Robert Edeson
Prince Dimitri Orlaff	Victor Varconi
Mariusha, a Gypsy	Julia Faye
Stefan, a Blacksmith	Theodore Kosloff
Vashi, a Boatman	Arthur Rankin

REVIEWS

"Here is a picture that both in story and treatment gets well away from the beaten path, but in its construction maintains the essential elements of audience interest and box-office appeal. A story of the Russian revolution, it is handled differently from any other of its kind. Mr. DeMille champions neither side in the conflict; each is shown as having its faults and virtues; nor are the characters of either hero or heroine overly sugar-coated to gain unalloyed sympathy; as a consequence, they are real, their actions more true to life, and their rather implausible romance more convincing."

> C. S. Sewell in
> *The Moving Picture World,*
> April 27, 1926.

"This picture from artistic and box-office standpoint looks to be about as good as anything that Cecil B. DeMille has ever done. That is taking in a lot of territory, but in this particular instance DeMille has turned out a picture that has a lot of that quality known to the trade as 'guts.' It is not one of the wishy-washy type of society mellers with bedrooms and bathrooms that have been his wont at times."

> The Weekly *Variety,*
> April 21, 1926.

Elinor Fair and William Boyd

William Boyd, Arthur Rankin, and Elinor Fair

Victor Varconi, Julia Faye, and DeMille

Jacqueline Logan

THE KING OF KINGS

Produced and directed by Cecil B. DeMille. Scenario by Jeanie Macpherson, adapted from the Four Gospels in the Holy Bible. Cameraman: J. Peverell Marley. Film Editors: Anne Bauchens, Harold McLernon. Musical Setting: Hugh Riesenfeld. Released by Pathé Exchange, Inc., April 19, 1927. Eighteen reels.

STORY

Mary Magdalene, a courtesan, is incensed when her newest admirer, Judas Iscariot, fails to attend a feast at her house; she hears that he has become a follower of one Jesus of Nazareth. In all her splendor, she goes to look upon this stranger. Yet when Jesus looks upon her, she is repentant, and He casts the seven devils from her, so that she too forsakes her wanton ways and becomes a follower of His. The familiar biblical episodes in the life of the Christus are thereafter enacted from the time He emerged as the teacher of Christianity as related in the Gospels, dramatizing His teachings and conversions, His betrayal and trial, His Crucifixion and Resurrection.

251

(Opposite page) Clayton Packard and Charles Requa

Andre Cherron, Lucia Flamma,
and Bryant Washburn

Joseph Schildkraut,
Jacqueline Logan, and players

CAST

Jesus, the Christ	H. B. Warner	*Procula, Wife of Pilate*	Majel Coleman
Mary, the Mother	Dorothy Cumming	*The Roman Centurion*	Montagu Love
The Twelve Disciples:		*Simon of Cyrene*	William Boyd
Peter	Ernest Torrence	*Mark*	M. Moore
Judas	Joseph Schildkraut	*Malchus, Captain of Guards*	Theodore Kosloff
James	James Neill	*Barabbas*	George Seigmann
John	Joseph Striker	*Martha*	Julia Faye
Matthew	Robert Edeson	*Mary of Bethany*	Josephine Norman
Thomas	Sidney D'Albrook	*Lazarus*	Kenneth Thomson
Andrew	David Imboden	*Satan*	Alan Brooks
Philip	Charles Belcher	*The Woman Taken*	
Bartholomew	Clayton Packard	*in Adultery*	Viola Louie
Simon	Robert Ellsworth	*The Blind Girl*	Muriel McCormac
James, the Less	Charles Requa	*Dysmas,*	
Thaddeus	John T. Prince	*the Repentant Thief*	Clarence Burton
Mary Magdalene	Jacqueline Logan	*Gestas, the Unrepentant*	
Caiaphas, High Priest		*Thief*	James Mason
of Israel	Rudolph Schildkraut	*The Mother of Gestas*	May Robson
The Pharisee	Sam DeGrasse	*Maidservant to Caiaphas*	Dot Farley
The Scribe	Casson Ferguson	*The Galilean Carpenter*	Hector Sarno
Pontius Pilate	Victor Varconi	*The Imbecile Boy*	Leon Holmes

Guests of Mary Magdalene:

Eber, a Pharisee	Otto Lederer
A Young Roman	Bryant Washburn
A Roman Noble	Lionel Belmore
A Rich Judaean	Monte Collins
A Gallant of Galilee	Luca Flamma
A Prince of Persia	Sojin
A Wealthy Merchant	Andre Cherron
A Babylonian Noble	William Costello
Slave to Mary Magdalene	Sally Rand
Charioteer	Noble Johnson
Captain of the Roman Guard	Jack Padgen
An Executioner	James Farley

Also in the cast, among many others: Robert St. Angelo, Joe Bonomo, Ed Brady, Charles Clary, Colin Chase, Fred Huntley, Brandon Hurst, George Marion, Louis Natheaux, Robert Ober, Louis Payne, Edward Piel, Josef Swickard, Carl Stockdale, Charles West, Stanhope Wheatcroft, Emily Barrye, Edna Mae Cooper, Josephine Crowell, Millie Davenport, Dale Fuller, Winifred Greenwood, Julia Swayne Gordon, Eulalie Jensen, Jane Keckley, Lydia Knott, Hedwig Reicher, Barbara Tennant, Mabel Van Buren.

H. B. Warner (the Christ) and Viola Lovie (the Woman Taken in Adultry)

Jacqueline Logan, Dorothy Cumming, and players — THE CRUCIFIXION

THE LAST SUPPER: H. B. Warner as the Christ

REVIEWS

"*The King of Kings* looks predestined to provoke many and strong arguments, according to the faith, and likely of all faiths. If achieving that end, and it may have been an aim, although the picture has been scrupulously produced to prevent adverse religious criticism, this DeMille celluloid monument will be a super-production for years to come. It should be, for the effort, the nerve, the investment and the results are entitled to that and more. . . . *The King of Kings* will live forever, on the screen and in memory."

The Weekly *Variety*,
April 20, 1927.

Josephine Norman (Mary), Kenneth Thomson (Lazarus), Julia Faye (Martha), and H. B. Warner (the Christ)

"So reverential is the spirit of Cecil B. DeMille's ambitious pictorial transcription of the life of Jesus of Nazareth, the Man, that during its initial screening at the Gaiety Theatre last Monday evening, hardly a whispered word was uttered among the audience. This production is entitled *The King of Kings*, and it is, in fact, the most impressive of all motion pictures."

Mordaunt Hall in
The New York Times,
April 20, 1927.

"The Supreme theme has been used. Jesus has come to the screen and DeMille has given us a picture which will tend to standardize the world's conception of the New Testament. It was a great thing that Cecil DeMille conceived and executed—something that will live for a long, long time and which will gross more money than any other picture ever made. DeMille has one of the best business minds in pictures and making *King of Kings* was the most brilliant stroke of his successful business career."

Welford Beaton in
The Film Spectator,
June 11, 1927.

Lina Basquette and Marie Prevost

Lina Basquette

Lina Basquette and George Duryea

Marie Prevost

THE GODLESS GIRL

Produced and directed by Cecil B. DeMille. Original scenario by Jeanie Macpherson, with Titles and Dialogue Sequences by Beulah Marie Dix and Jeanie Macpherson. Cameraman: J. Peverell Marley. Film Editor: Anne Bauchens. Released by Pathé Exchange, Inc., March 31, 1929. Twelve reels.

STORY

A group of high school students, led by the Girl and the Boy, turn from Christian teaching as old-fashioned, and hold secret atheistic meetings. They are raided, and an innocent girl is killed accidentally when a stairway collapses. The Girl and the Boy are put in reform school, and subjected to every brutality. But they regain faith in God, and the Boy proves his newfound belief when he rescues not only the Girl from a burning building, but also the Brute who had so mistreated him.

257

CAST

The Girl	Lina Basquette
The Other Girl	Marie Prevost
The Boy	George Duryea
The Brute	Noah Beery
The Goat	Eddie Quillan
The Victim	Mary Jane Irving
The Matrons	Gertrude Quality
	Kate Price
	Hedwig Reicher
The Inmates	Julia Faye
	Viola Louie
	Emily Barrye
	Jacqueline Dyrese
The Guards	Clarence Burton
	Dick Alexander

George Duryea and Lina Basquette

George Duryea and Lina Basquette

Marie Prevost

George Duryea, Noah Beery, and Lina Basquette

Marie Prevost and Lina Basquette

REVIEWS

"Cecil B. DeMille had his tongue in his cheek when he directed this hack yarn with religious undercurrents. He was ogling for favor in the same direction as *King of Kings* and possibly at the start contemplated a pretentious production. Long delay in bringing the picture into New York indicates weaknesses were appreciated with the hold-out for the purpose of adding dialogue. Talk may help the ballyhoo. It does not enhance the entertainment and is so palpably unnecessary that laymen are apt to sense this even if lacking the trade knowledge to define the flaws."

The Weekly *Variety*,
April 3, 1929.

"A surprising piece of romantic evangelism is *The Godless Girl*. The story, which stretches from unexpected ludicrous slapstick through scenes in a burning reformatory, the intensity in feeling of which equals motion picture depictions of the French revolution, is punctured with vapid, religious admonitions and strange, heavenly warnings in the form of crosses burnt into the palms of the heroine. . . . Cecil B. DeMille directed the film, and while it has some commendable dramatic moments, its effectiveness is blunted by the introduction of unwarranted, slapstick comedy . . . . The two last scenes are in dialogue, but serve no appreciable purpose."

Mordaunt Hall in
The New York Times,
April 1, 1929.

Eddie Quillan and Lina Basquette

Marie Prevost and Lina Basquette

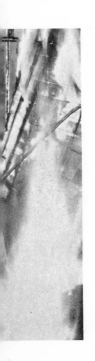

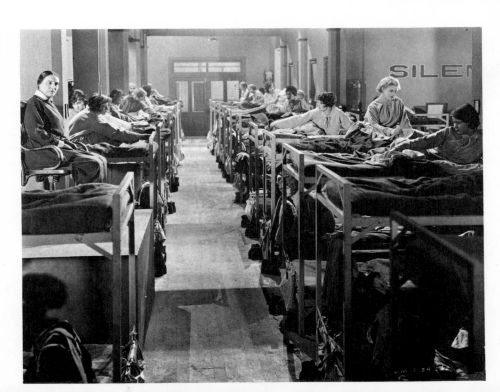

259

PART 2

THE
SOUND FILMS

Julia Faye, Kay Johnson, Conrad Nagel, and Joel McCrea

Charles Bickford, Kay Johnson,
Muriel McCormac, and Clarence Burton

Joel McCrea, Julia Faye, and Kay Johnson

Julia Faye, Kay Johnson, Charles Bickford, and Conrad Nagel

Julia Faye and Joel McCrea

DYNAMITE

Produced and directed by Cecil B. DeMille. Original screenplay by Jeanie Macpherson. Dialogue by John Howard Lawson, Gladys Unger, and Jeanie Macpherson. Cameraman: J. Peverell Marley. Film Editor: Anne Bauchens. Music: Herbert Stothart. Theme Song, "How Am I to Know?" by Dorothy Parker. Released by Metro-Goldwyn-Mayer Distributing Corp., December 13, 1929. Fourteen reels.

STORY

Cynthia Crothers, a socialite, in order to comply with a will leaving her millions so that she may buy another woman's husband whom she thinks she loves, weds a miner, Hagon Derk, who has been condemned to death for murder.

Although Cynthia marries him on the very eve of his execution, Hagon is saved at the eleventh hour, and Cynthia is stuck with a husband who detests her and calls her worthless. He returns to work in the mines, and because she must be living with him on a certain date, she journeys to the mining town and persuades him to let her move in for a few days as his lawful wife. There is a disastrous mine catastrophe, and Cynthia, her husband Derk, and her lover Roger Towne are trapped beneath the earth. The lover proves himself a hero by exploding a stick of dynamite so that they may escape. Roger is killed, but Cynthia finds that in her rough miner husband she has gained a mate worthy of her love.

CAST

Cynthia Crothers	Kay Johnson
Hagon Derk	Charles Bickford
Roger Towne	Conrad Nagel
Marcia Towne	Julia Faye
Katie Derk	Muriel McCormac
Marco, the "Sheik"	Joel McCrea
Three Wise Fools	Robert Edeson
	William Holden
	Henry Stockbridge
Young Vultures	Leslie Fenton
	Barton Hepburn
Good Mixers	Ernest Hilliard
	June Nash
	Nancy Dover
	Neely Edwards
	Jerry Zier
	Rita LeRoy
The Life of the Party	Tyler Brooke
Officers	Clarence Burton
	James Farley
The Judge	Robert T. Haines
Bobby	Douglas Frazer Scott
His Mother	Jane Keckley
Neighbors	Blanche Craig
	Mary Gordon
	Ynez Seabury
Radio Announcer	Scott Kolk
The Doctor	Fred Walton

Charles Bickford, DeMille, and Kay Johnson

REVIEWS

"A pot-pourri of about all previous DeMille efforts crammed into one picture. Held up by the excellence of the individual performances, the lavish production and a mine cave-in climax. Picture is sure-fire box-office fare and is a likely holdover entry for some spots, despite its unnecessary length .... Those familiar with DeMille's

Charles Bickford and Kay Johnson

work will see almost a resume of his entire screen directing career in this society picture heavily seasoned with dramatic hoke."

The Weekly *Variety*,
January 1, 1930.

"In *Dynamite*, Cecil B. DeMille's first entry in the talking picture field, this producer evidently is undaunted by the vocal angle of his film, for he pursues much the same tactics he did in his silent contributions. As in the past, he proves himself to be a master of technical detail and a director who is able to elicit from his players thoroughly competent performances. Nevertheless, this offering is an astonishing mixture, with artificiality vying with realism and comedy hanging on the heels of grim melodrama."

Mordaunt Hall in
The New York Times,
December 28, 1929.

Conrad Nagel, Kay Johnson, Joel McCrea, and Julia Faye

Kay Johnson, Conrad Nagel,
and Charles Bickford

Kay Johnson—in a DeMille bathroom

The end of the party in the dirigible

MADAME SATAN

Produced and directed by Cecil B. DeMille. Original screenplay by Jeanie Macpherson. Dialogue by Gladys Unger and Elsie Janis. Cameraman: Harold Rosson. Film Editor: Anne Bauchens. Music and Lyrics by Clifford Grey, Herbert Stothart, Elsie Janis, Jack King. Released by Metro-Goldwyn-Mayer Distributing Corp., October 5, 1930. Thirteen reels.

STORY

Socialite Angela Brooks knows she is losing her husband Bob's love to a gay young creature known as Trixie. Advised by her maid, Angela takes on a new personality, and becomes known as the mysterious "Madam Satan," out to fascinate and recapture her own husband. At a costume ball held aboard a giant dirigible, Bob Brooks admits he is absolutely entranced with "Madam Satan." When the dirigible is struck by lightning and catches fire, Angela gives her parachute to the distraught Trixie. Bob gives Angela his own parachute, and falls with the dirigible wreck, managing to dive at the last moment into the Central Park reservoir, thereby preserving himself for the delectable Angela, alias "Madam Satan."

Reginald Denny and Kay Johnson

Theodore Kosloff and the "Ballet Mechanique"

CAST

Angela Brooks	Kay Johnson
Bob Brooks	Reginald Denny
Trixie	Lillian Roth
Jimmy Wade	Roland Young
Martha	Elsa Peterson
Captain	Boyd Irwin
First Mate	Wallace MacDonald
A Roman Senator	Wilfred Lucas
Romeo	Tyler Brooke
Eve	Lotus Thompson
Call of the Wild	Vera Marsh
Fish Girl	Martha Sleeper
Water	Doris McMahon
Confusion	Marie Valli
Miss Conning Tower	Julanne Johnston
Empire Officer	Albert Conti
Pirate	Earl Askam
Little Rolls Riding Hood	Betty Francisco
Babo	Ynez Seabury
Spain	Countess De Liguoro
Spider Girl	Katherine Irving
Victory	Aileen Ransom
Electricity	
(Ballet Mechanique)	Theodore Kosloff
Herman	Jack King
Riff	Edward Prinz
Abe Lyman and His Band	

REVIEWS

"Cecil B. DeMille's latest audible film, *Madam Satan*, which is now at the Capitol, is a strange conglomeration of unreal incidents that are sometimes set forth with no little technical skill. It begins with the flash of a bird-bath and closes with the parachuting of passengers from a giant dirigible that is struck by lightning.... It is an inept story with touches of comedy that are more tedious than laughable."

Mordaunt Hall in
The New York Times,
October 6, 1930.

"DeMille is still the master of the circusy exploit. He discloses this in *Madam Satan* when to the accompaniment of a veritable pandemonium he smashes up a Zeppelin and sends a throng of masquerade dancers hurtling into midair in parachutes.... The general impression of the DeMille picture is that it is too much in one key. The superabundance of sound palls, and leaves one weary. Besides, there is a staginess about the whole result that casts anything approaching conviction to one side."

Edwin Schallert in
The Los Angeles Times,
September 26, 1930.

Reginald Denny, Lillian Roth, and Roland Young

DeMille and daughter Katherine

Roland Young, Lillian Roth, and Reginald Denny

Lupe Velez

Warner Baxter
and Eleanor Boardman

THE SQUAW MAN

Produced and directed by Cecil B. DeMille. (Entitled in England, The White Man.) Screenplay by Lucien Hubbard and Lenore J. Coffee, adapted from the play by Edwin Milton Royle. Dialogue by Elsie Janis. Cameraman: Harold Rosson. Film Editor: Anne Bauchens. Music: Herbert Stothart. Released by Metro-Goldwyn-Mayer Distributing Corp., September 19, 1931. Twelve reels.

STORY

In story, DeMille's talking version remains essentially the same as the two previous ones he filmed in 1914 and again in 1918.

Warner Baxter and DeWitt Jennings

Charles Bickford and Warner Baxter

Paul Cavanagh, Warner Baxter, Roland Young, and DeMille

CAST

Jim Wynn	Warner Baxter
Naturich	Lupe Velez
Diana	Eleanor Boardman
Lord Henry Kerhill	Paul Cavanagh
General Stafford	Lawrence Grant
Sir John Applegate	Roland Young
Cash Hawkins	Charles Bickford
Hardwick	Desmond Roberts
Tabywanna	Mitchell Lewis
Shanks	Luke Cosgrove
Bill	J. Farrell MacDonald
Sheriff	DeWitt Jennings
Grouchy	Frank Rice
Shorty	Raymond Hatton
Clerk	Frank Hagney
Andy	Victor Potel
Hal	Dickie Moore
Butler	Harry Northrup
Mrs. Jones	Julia Faye
Henry's Mother	Eva Dennison
McSorley	Ed Brady
Babs	Lillian Bond

REVIEWS

"And now in its twenty-sixth year, Mr. DeMille has taken up *The Squaw Man* again, spinning about its miscegenetic tale of fortitude and sorrow a production that is taking close to two hours to present at the Capitol. Skilfully acted by a dozen good players, handsomely produced as to scenery and technical excellence, it makes an interesting entertainment—one that is too somber in its story to be called amusing and too neatly carpentered in its plot to be called genuine tragedy. The seams of age shine through; it is agreeable and expert melodrama."

Mordaunt Hall in
The New York Times,
September 19, 1931.

"There's everything in this version that has been in former ones, only it is more plausibly done. Warner Baxter does a magnificent job. Lupe Velez, with scarcely a dozen words of dialogue, holds sympathy every second. Eleanor Boardman, Charles Bickford, and Raymond Hatton offer excellent support. See it, no matter if you have already seen it on the stage or silent screen."

Photoplay Magazine,
August, 1931.

Eleanor Boardman, Warner Baxter, Winifred Kingston, and DeMille

Charles Bickford

Warner Baxter, Eleanor Boardman, and Paul Cavanagh

Lupe Velez

Elissa Landi and Mickey Moore

278

Charles Laughton, Claudette Colbert, and Fredric March

THE SIGN OF THE CROSS

Produced and directed by Cecil B. DeMille. Screenplay by Waldemar Young and Sidney Buchman, adapted from the play by Wilson Barrett. Cameraman: Karl Struss. Film Editor: Anne Bauchens. Music: Rudolph Kopp. Released by the Paramount Publix Corp., December 3, 1932. Fourteen reels.

STORY

Mercia, a Christian maid in ancient Rome, is desired by the Prefect of Rome, Marcus Superbus, but she will not give way to his desires. To humiliate her, Marcus confines her with a notorious lesbian, Ancaria, who also gets nowhere. Meanwhile, the Empress Poppaea tries to seduce Marcus, but with no success. The half-mad Emperor Nero sets Rome on fire, and blames the Christians for the conflagration, so they are rounded up and led to the Colisseum for slaughter. Mercia's strength of will and sublime faith so intrigue Marcus that he realizes he has truly fallen in love with her, and when she is led into the arena to be fed to the lions, he renounces his pagan gods to join her in death.

Fredric March and Claudette Colbert

Joyzelle Joyner, Elissa Landi, and Fredric March

280

CAST

Marcus Superbus	Fredric March
Mercia	Elissa Landi
Poppaea	Claudette Colbert
Nero	Charles Laughton
Tigellinus	Ian Keith
Dacia	Vivian Tobin
Favius	Harry Beresford
Glabrio	Ferdinand Gottschalk
Titus	Arthur Hohl
Ancaria	Joyzelle Joyner
Stephanus	Tommy Conlon
Strabo	Nat Pendleton
Licinius	William V. Mong
Tyros	Harold Healy
Viturius	Robert Alexander
Philodemus	Robert Manning
The Mule Giant	Joe Bonomo

Also in the cast, among many others: Lillian Leighton, Otto Lederer, Lane Chandler, Wilfred Lucas, Jerome Storm, Florence Turner, Gertrude Norman, Horace B. Carpenter, Carol Holloway, Ynez Seabury.

Claudette Colbert and DeMille

Fredric March

Charles Laughton

"DeMille staged his spectacle in his customary way, turning in a job that for sight stuff hasn't been duplicated since the silent picture days. His eye for extravagant production effects and secret of getting the most out of mobs so as to make a regiment look like an army, have not left him. Mrs. Nero's (Miss Colbert) bath in a pool of asses' milk just gives a slight hint."

The Weekly *Variety*,
December 6, 1932.

"No DeMille picture would be complete without some suggestion of a bathtub, and here this director goes himself one better by having a small swimming pool filled with the milk of asses. It is the wont of Nero's wife, Poppaea, to revel in this pool, and as another touch from the master of Hollywood, one beholds first one cat, and then another beside the pool lapping up the milk. If Wilson Barrett could only have seen it!"

Mordaunt Hall in
The New York Times,
December 1, 1932.

Elissa Landi and Fredric March

Richard Cromwell, Charles Bickford, and cast

Judith Allen and Richard Cromwell

Bradley Page and Charles Bickford

THIS DAY AND AGE

Produced and directed by Cecil B. DeMille. Original screenplay by Bartlett Cormack. Cameraman: J. Peverell Marley. Film Editor: Anne Bauchens. Music: Howard Jackson, L. W. Gilbert, and Abel Baer. Released by Paramount Productions, Inc., August 25, 1933. Nine reels.

STORY

On the day the boys of a certain city assume civic governmental jobs for a day, Garrett, a gangster, kills the boys' presser and tailor. The boys, led by Steve Smith, know Garrett is guilty, but the defense attorney gets Garrett free. The boys try to incriminate Garrett, and are forced to kidnap him, taking him to an abandoned brickyard, where by gangster torture methods, they force a confession from the terrified criminal. Through the actions of the girl, Gay Merrick, police are diverted to the brickyard when other gangsters gang up to save their leader, and so a massacre is averted. The boys triumph, and Steve and Gay are the hero and heroine of the hour.

CAST

Garrett	Charles Bickford
Gay Merrick	Judith Allen
Steve Smith	Richard Cromwell
Herman	Harry Green
Don Merrick	Eddie Nugent
Morry Dover	Ben Alexander
Gus	Oscar Rudolph
Manager of Night Club	Billy Gilbert
Sam Weber	Lester Arnold
Max	Fuzzy Knight
The Sheriff	Wade Boteler
Toledo	Bradley Page
Mr. Smith	Harry C. Bradley
Mrs. Smith	Louise Carter
Billy Anderson	Michael Stuart
Chief of Police	Guy Usher
Judge McGuire	George Barbier
District Attorney	Charles Middleton
Defense Attorney	Warner Richmond
George Harris	Onest Conly
Mayor	Samuel S. Hinds
Mosher	Mickey Daniels
City Editor	Howard Lang
Little Fellow	Arthur Vinton
Little Fellow's Mother	Nella Walker

Charles Bickford

Bradley Page, Richard Cromwell, and cast

Charles Bickford, Richard Cromwell, and Eddie Nugent

Eddie Nugent, Charles Bickford, and Richard Cromwell

REVIEWS

"Treating a daring topic, modern American high school youth toppling over every established judicial procedure, going to the mat with gangsterism and taking the law into its own hands, *This Day and Age* is unquestionably a sensational and courageous picture. Its predominant audience value is that it is loaded with that power that excites emotional hysteria. There is nothing dainty about it. It's starkly realistic to the last degree. Undoubtedly, because of the way in which it ties high school boys in with its subject, it will precipitate controversy. Yet due to the manner in which DeMille has built up his story, the way in which he has handled mobs of frenzied youths to obtain spectacle, together with the method in which he has adapted patriotic music to inspire audiences, there is something sublime about the show that should stimulate audiences to the same pitch of enthusiasm that it did the preview crowd."

McCarthy in
The Motion Picture Herald,
July 29, 1933.

"A strange tale from the Hollywood hills. . . . The technical work on the production is beyond reproach, but the story is excessively melodramatic."

Mordaunt Hall in
The New York Times,
August 26, 1933.

287

Claudette Colbert

Mary Boland, Claudette Colbert,
Herbert Marshall,
and William Gargan

288

Claudette Colbert

FOUR FRIGHTENED PEOPLE

Produced and directed by Cecil B. DeMille. Screenplay by Bartlett Cormack and Lenore J. Coffee, adapted from the novel by E. Arnot Robertson. Cameraman: Karl Struss. Film Editor: Anne Bauchens. Music: Karl Hajos, Milton Roder, H. Rohenheld, and John Leipold. Released by Paramount Productions, Inc., January 27, 1934. Eight reels.

STORY

Four frightened people—a rubber chemist, a Chicago geography teacher, a British official's wife, and a newspaper correspondent—are thrown together when there is an outbreak of the bubonic plague aboard a Dutch Coastal steamer carrying them from their ports of embarkation back to civilization. The four shanghai a lifeboat, and, led by a half-caste guide, they tramp through the perilous jungle, where they are attacked by a pygmy tribe and encounter all manner of jungle danger—and some of them eventually reach safety, very different people.

289

CAST

Judy Cavendish	Claudette Colbert
Arnold Ainger	Herbert Marshall
Mrs. Mardick	Mary Boland
Stewart Corder	William Gargan
Montague	Leo Carrillo
Mrs. Ainger	Nella Walker
Native Chief	Tetsu Komai
Native Boatman	Chris Pin Martin
Native	Joe De La Cruz
Four Sakais	Minoru Nisheda
	Toru Shimada
	E. R. Jinedas
	Delmar Costello

REVIEWS

"It is an extravagant mixture of comedy and melodrama, and the terror in some of the scenes stirred up almost as much mirth from an audience yesterday afternoon as did the levity in others. . . . Even in this narrative, Mr. DeMille indulges his fancy for showing persons bathing, if not for bathtubs. Claudette Colbert, who plays Judith, hangs her clothes on a hickory limb and they are purloined by a monkey, which gives the producer the chance of showing how useful as clothing huge tropical leaves can be in an emergency. Subsequently, Judith succeeds in getting a nice, neat suit of leopard skin."

Mordaunt Hall in
The New York Times,
January 27, 1934.

"The DeMillean bathtub penchant evidences itself even in the jungle when Miss Colbert, sans cheaters and very Eve (when a playful chimpanzee steals her clothes), emerges with plenty of s.a. for both men."

The Weekly *Variety*,
January 30, 1934.

Claudette Colbert

Claudette Colbert, Herbert Marshall, and William Gargan

290

Mary Boland

Claudette Colbert

Claudette Colbert and Henry Wilcoxon

Henry Wilcoxon

CLEOPATRA

Produced and directed by Cecil B. DeMille. Screenplay by Waldemar Young and Vincent Lawrence, from an adaptation by Waldemar Young. Cameraman: Victor Milner. Film Editor: Anne Bauchens. Music: Rudolph Kopp. Presented by Adolph Zukor. Released by Paramount Productions, Inc., July 25, 1934. Eleven reels.

STORY

Julius Caesar is infatuated with Egypt's Queen Cleopatra, and is especially conscious of her country's wealth. He brings Cleopatra to Rome when he returns, planning to divorce his wife, set himself up as king and dictator, and then wed the Egyptian queen. But Caesar is assassinated, and Cleopatra flees to Egypt, where Marc Antony goes to return her in chains to Rome. But Antony also falls a victim to her charms, and is denounced in Rome as a traitor. Antony joins the Egyptians in a fight against the Romans, and at the naval Battle of Actium the Romans defeat the Egyptians. Marc Antony commits suicide, and Cleopatra dies of the bite of a poisonous asp rather than go back to Rome, a prisoner.

Ian MacLaren, Leonard Mudde, Edward Maxwell,
Arthur Hohl, and Thomas Morris

Warren William

CAST

Cleopatra	Claudette Colbert	*Brutus*	Arthur Hohl
Julius Caesar	Warren William	*Pothinos*	Leonard Mudie
Marc Antony	Henry Wilcoxon	*Appollodorus*	Irving Pichel
Calpurnia	Gertrude Michael	*Octavia*	Claudia Dell
Herod	Joseph Schildkraut	*Charmian*	Eleanor Phelps
Octavius	Ian Keith	*Drussus*	John Rutherford
Enobarbus	C. Aubrey Smith	*Iras*	Grace Durkin
Cassius	Ian MacLaren	*Achillas*	Robert Warwick
		Casca	Edwin Maxwell
		Cicero	Charles Morris
		The Soothsayer	Harry Beresford

Claudette Colbert

"DeMille adds nothing to his directorial rep in this one, other than to again demonstrate his rare skill in the handling of mass action. He offers nothing new in this direction, though he does provide one of the finest examples of rhythm in a picture yet to be exploited. This comes when the barge of Cleopatra moves out of the port to carry the enchantress and Marc Antony to Egypt."

The Weekly *Variety*,
August 21, 1934.

"Mr. DeMille has here contrived a film which reflects many of the influences of William Shakespeare and George Bernard Shaw and at the same time is filled with modern, easy-going dialogue.... It is worthy of note that there is virtually nothing in the picture which could be described as offensive. In fact, Mr. DeMille depicts a surprisingly moral life in the Roman and Egyptian courts."

"Ayer" in
The Motion Picture Herald,
August 25, 1934.

Warren William and Gertrude Michael

Henry Wilcoxon

296

Warren William, Claudette Colbert, and players

Claudette Colbert

Alan Hale and Loretta Young

Loretta Young and Henry Wilcoxon

THE CRUSADES

Produced and directed by Cecil B. DeMille. Screenplay by Harold Lamb, Waldemar Young, and Dudley Nichols. Cameraman: Victor Milner. Film Editor: Anne Bauchens. Music: Rudolph Kopp. Lyrics by Harold Lamb. Presented by Adolph Zukor for release by Paramount Productions, Inc., August 21, 1935. Thirteen reels.

STORY

A holy man known as The Hermit arouses all the kings and princes of medieval Europe in a crusade to wrest dominion of Jerusalem and the Holy Sepulchre from the Saracens. Richard the Lion-Hearted, King of England, having spurned the French princess Alice, accepts betrothal to Berengaria, whom he has never seen, in return for subsistence for the Crusade, and she is formally married to his sword. The crusading knights and their armies march upon the infidel Saladin, who has captured Berengaria, and is holding her a prisoner. In the end it is Saladin who opens the gates of Jerusalem to all Christians everywhere who come in peace. Only one

299

man does Saladin bar from entry into the city—Richard the Lion-Hearted, who had vowed he would rest his conquering sword on the Holy Sepulchre. But Saladin does relinquish Berengaria to Richard so that she may return with him to England as his Queen.

CAST

Berengaria	Loretta Young
Richard the Lion-Hearted	Henry Wilcoxon
Saladin	Ian Keith
The Hermit	C. Aubrey Smith
Alice of France	Katherine DeMille
Conrad of Montferrat	Joseph Schildkraut
Blondel	Alan Hale
Philip of France	C. Henry Gordon
Sancho, King of Navarre	George Barbier
The Blacksmith	Montagu Love
Robert, Earl of Leicester	Lumsden Hare
Hugo, Duke of Burgundy	William Farnum
Frederick, Duke of the Germans	Hobart Bosworth
Karakush	Pedro de Cordoba
John, Prince of England	Ramsay Hill
Monk	Mischa Auer
Alan, Richard's Squire	Maurice Murphy
Amir	Jason Robards
Arab Slave-Seller	J. Carroll Naish
Philip's Squire	Oscar Rudolph
Leopold, Duke of Austria	Albert Conti
Sverre, the Norse King	Sven-Hugo Borg
Michael, Prince of Russia	Paul Satoff
William, King of Sicily	Fred Malatesta
Nicholas, Count of Hungary	Hans Von Twardowski
Duenna	Anna Demetrio
Soldier	Perry Askam
Ship's Master	Edwin Maxwell
Archbishop	Winter Hall
Mother of Alan	Emma Dunn
Nun	Georgia Caine
English Chamberlain	Robert Adair
Leicester's Squire	Pat Moore
Christian Girl	Ann Sheridan
Buyer	Josef Swickard
Christian Girl	Jean Fenwick
Cart Man	Edgar Dearing
Priest	Alphonse Ethier
1st Lady-in-Waiting to Alice	Gilda Oliva
2nd Lady-in-Waiting to Alice	Mildred Van Buren
Knight	John Rutherford
Stranger (Messenger)	Colin Tapley
Amir	Harry Cording
Amir	Stanley Andrews
Sentry	Addison Richards
Amir	Maurice Black
Amir	William B. Davidson
Grey Beard	Guy Usher
Templar	Boyd Irwin
Captain of English Men-at-Arms	Kenneth Gibson
Templar	Gordon Griffith
Templar	Guy Usher
Chanting Monk	Vallejo Gantner
Captain of Templars	George MacQuarrie
Captain of Hospitalers	Sam Flint
Wounded Man	Harold Goodwin

Henry Wilcoxon and players

"Synonymous always with all that the name Cecil B. DeMille stands for in relation to mighty, colorful pageantry and spectacle, massive settings and accoutrements, it tells a story that will never die. It is the composite story of several of the early Crusades. It's an inspiring martial story, powerful, but humanly understandable, that transcends all racial or religious prejudices."

McCarthy in
The Motion Picture Herald,
August 10, 1935.

"Mr. DeMille has no peer in the world when it comes to bringing the panoplied splendor of the

Joseph Schildkraut and Katherine DeMille

past into torrential life upon the screen. *The Crusades* presents him at the top of his achievement, with the virtues of his method towering majestically above his obvious faults.... At its best, *The Crusades* possesses the true quality of a screen epic. It is rich in the kind of excitement that pulls an audience irresistibly to the edge of its seat."

André Sennwald in
The New York Times,
August 22, 1935.

"Cinemaddicts who have had 20 years in which to grow accustomed to the methods of Cecil Blount DeMille by now have some idea what to expect in a DeMille version of the Holy Wars. *The Crusades* should fulfill all expectations. As a picture it is historically worthless, didactically treacherous, artistically absurd. None of these defects impairs its entertainment value. It is a $100,000,000 sideshow which has at least three features which distinguish it from the long line of previous DeMille extravaganzas. It is the noisiest; it is the biggest; it contains no baths."

Time,
September 2, 1935.

Henry Wilcoxon

Joseph Schildkraut, Lumsden Hare, Katherine DeMille, and Henry Wilcoxon

Loretta Young

Jean Arthur, Gary Cooper, and James Ellison

Gary Cooper (*on floor*), Porter Hall, and Jean Arthur

James Ellison and players

THE PLAINSMAN

Produced and directed by Cecil B. DeMille. Screenplay by Waldemar Young, Harold Lamb, and Lynn Riggs, based on an unpublished original screen story by Courtney Riley Cooper, the book Wild Bill Hickok *by Frank J. Wilstach, and material compiled by Jeanie Macpherson. Cameramen: Victor Milner and George Robinson. Film Editor: Anne Bauchens. Original Music: George Antheil. Executive Producer: William LeBaron. Presented by Adolph Zukor for release by Paramount Pictures, Inc., January 1, 1937. Twelve reels.*

STORY

Wild Bill Hickok, determined to bring a new civilization to the American frontier, is the bitter enemy of John Lattimer, a renegade gun-runner. Hickok's great friendship with Buffalo Bill is imperilled when Hickok is forced to turn outlaw before he can come to a final show-down with Lattimer. Hickok is loved by Calamity Jane, but he never admits he even cares for her until the double-dealing Jack McCall shoots him. Wild Bill dies in Calamity Jane's arms, and she gives him a last kiss he'll never be able to wipe off.

Victor Varconi, Paul Harvey,
Gary Cooper, and Jean Arthur

Gary Cooper and Jean Arthur

CAST

Wild Bill Hickok	Gary Cooper
Calamity Jane	Jean Arthur
Buffalo Bill Cody	James Ellison
John Lattimer	Charles Bickford
Louisa Cody	Helen Burgess
Jack McCall	Porter Hall
Yellow Hand	Paul Harvey
Painted Horse	Victor Varconi
General George A. Custer	John Miljan
Abraham Lincoln	Frank McGlyn
Van Ellyn	Granville Bates
Young Trooper	Frank Albertson
Captain Wood	Purnell Pratt
Jake	Fred Kohler, Sr.
Breezy	George Hayes
Dave	Fuzzy Knight
Sergeant McGinnis	Pat Moriarty
Tony, the Barber	Charles Judels
Quartermaster Sergeant	Harry Woods
A Cheyenne Indian	Anthony Quinn
A River Gambler	Francis J. McDonald
Boy on the Dock	George Ernest
General Merritt	George MacQuarrie
A Courier from Custer	Edgar Dearing
Stanton, Secretary of War	Edwin Maxwell
Purser of the 'Lizzie Gill'	Bruce Warren

REVIEWS

"Played with spirit and intelligent understanding by principals and entire supporting cast, with class individual performances sticking out all over and directed in the same style, all the substantiating features—locales, photography and particularly the musical accompaniment—have a definite place in the general scheme. All of them have been applied by DeMille to produce quality thrill and action entertainment, the exploitation values of which are limited only by how intensely showmen want to work and how much money they have to spend."

The Motion Picture Herald,
November 28, 1936.

"*The Plainsman* is a big and a good western. It should do all right for business, possibly irregular in spots, but ranging from big to good.... It's cowboys and Indians on a broad, sweeping scale; not a *Covered Wagon*, but realistic enough."

The Weekly *Variety,*
January 20, 1937.

James Ellison, George Hayes, and Gary Cooper

Gary Cooper and Jean Arthur

Anthony Quinn

Fredric March and Franciska Gaal

THE BUCCANEER

Produced and directed by Cecil B. DeMille. Screenplay by Edwin Justus Mayer, Harold Lamb, and C. Gardner Sullivan, based on an adaptation by Jeanie Macpherson of Lafitte the Pirate *by Lyle Saxon. Cameraman: Victor Milner. Film Editor: Anne Bauchens. Musical Score: George Antheil. Executive Producer: William LeBaron. Associate Producer: William H. Pine. Presented by Adolph Zukor for release by Paramount Pictures, Inc., February 4, 1938. Thirteen reels.*

STORY

Jean Lafitte, dashing pirate of the Louisiana bayous, is forced to hide away from his beloved New Orleans. He preys on all other country's ships which come in his way, but molests no packets flying the American flag. He is in love with a New Orleans socialite, Annette, but is loved by a little Dutch girl, Gretchen, whom he has rescued from a pirate-scuttled vessel. During the War of 1812, when it seems that the British may be victorious, Lafitte and his men come to the aid of General Jackson and his backwoodsmen, and save New Orleans for America.

309

(Opposite page) Fredric March and Akim Tamiroff

But at the Victory Ball, when Lafitte is honored and about to win the respect he has always craved, his fiancée Annette unwittingly reveals that Lafitte and his brigands had burned a boat carrying Annette's younger sister away on an elopement. Lafitte is thus forced again to desert New Orleans and seek refuge in the bayous with his men.

CAST

Jean Lafitte	Fredric March
Gretchen	Franciska Gaal
Dominique You	Akim Tamiroff
Annette	Margot Grahame
Ezra Peavey	Walter Brennan
Beluche	Anthony Quinn
Crawford	Ian Keith
Governor Claiborne	Douglass Dumbrille
Gramby	Fred Kohler, Sr.
Captain Brown	Robert Barrat
Andrew Jackson	Hugh Sothern
Mouse	John Rogers
Tarsus	Hans Steinke
Collector of Port	Stanley Andrews
Aunt Charlotte	Beulah Bondi
Dolly Madison	Spring Byington
Admiral Cockburn	Montagu Love
Marie de Remy	Louise Campbell
General Ross	Eric Stanley
Captain Lockyer	Gilbert Emery
Captain McWilliams	Holmes Herbert
Madeleine	Evelyn Keyes
Camden Blount	Francis J. McDonald
Lieut. Shreve	Frank Melton
Charles	Jack Hubbard
Captain Reid	Richard Denning
Roxane	Lina Basquette
Young Blade	John Patterson

Also in the cast, among others: Reginald Sheffield, Barry Norton, John Sutton, Mae Busch, Philo McCullough, Ethel Clayton, Jane Keckley, Maude Fealy, Charles Morton, Stanhope Wheatcroft, James Craig, Crauford Kent, Charlotte Wynters, E. J. LeSaint, Ed Brady, Ralph Lewis.

Beulah Bondi

Margot Grahame, Franciska Gaal, and Fredric March

Gilbert Emery and Fredric March

Fredric March and Margot Grahame

Fredric March, Akim Tamiroff, and Fred Kohlen, Sr.

Fredric March

Anthony Quinn, Fredric March, Franciska Gaal, and Akim Tamiroff

Akim Tamiroff and Fredric March

REVIEWS

"This is Mr. DeMille's twenty-fifth anniversary production, latest in that quarter of a century array of titles that began with *The Squaw Man* and the founding of Hollywood in 1913. From his skilled craftsmanship have come other pictures quite as ambitious, none more adroitly fabricated, skilfully adjusted to the norm of appeal to the world audience that such imposing and costly productions must command."

Terry Ramsaye in
The Motion Picture Herald,
January 15, 1938.

"DeMille, in again recoursing to American history, obviously recognized the necessity for adulterating fact with palatable celluloid fiction, and his scriveners have seen to it that both are well blended. In typical DeMille manner he broadly sweeps the spectacular on the screen, including not a little of the American flag stuff, which is stirringly fitting for the occasion, and yet at the same time the British sensitivities have been well preserved."

The Weekly *Variety,*
January 12, 1938.

Hugh Sothern, Fredric March,
and Douglas Dumbrille

Ian Keith and Fredric March

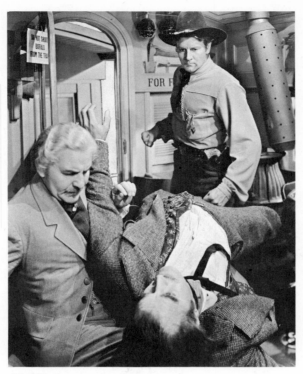

Joel McCrea

Brian Donlevy, Sheila Darcy, and Julia Faye

314

UNION PACIFIC

Produced and directed by Cecil B. DeMille. Screenplay by Walter DeLeon, C. Gardner Sullivan, and Jesse Lasky, Jr., adapted by Jack Cunningham from a novel, Trouble Shooter, *by Ernest Haycox. Cameraman: Victor Milner. Film Editor: Anne Bauchens. Music Score: Sigmund Krumgold and John Leipold. Executive Producer: William LeBaron. Associate Producer: William H. Pine. Released by Paramount Pictures, Inc., April 28, 1939. Fourteen reels.*

STORY

Jeff Butler is overseer for the building of the transcontinental railroad, the Union Pacific, and he meets and falls in love with Mollie Monahan, a railroad engineer's daughter and railroad postmistress. Dick Allen, gambler, a onetime pal of Butler's, is now in the employ of another gambler, Campeau, and they have been hired as saboteurs by a railroad politician secretly trying to impede the progress of the building of the Union Pacific. Dick Allen robs a company pay train, and is defended by Mollie, who persuades him to return the money. Dismissed from the postal service, Mollie meets with Jeff Butler and Dick Allen again on a train which is besieged by Indian raiders; they are saved by the United States Army, but Allen is slain by Campeau, who is also killed. The Union Pacific Railroad is completed by the driving of the golden spike at Promontory Point, and Butler and Mollie realize they are in love.

CAST

Mollie Monahan	Barbara Stanwyck
Jeff Butler	Joel McCrea
Fiesta	Akim Tamiroff
Dick Allen	Robert Preston
Leach Overmile	Lynne Overman
Sid Campeau	Brian Donlevy
Jack Cordray	Anthony Quinn
Mrs. Calvin	Evelyn Keyes
Duke Ring	Robert Barrat
Casement	Stanley Ridges
Asa M. Barrows	Henry Kolker
Grenville M. Dodge	Francis J. McDonald
Oakes Ames	Willard Robertson
Calvin	Harold Goodwin
Sam Reed	Richard Lane
Dusky Clayton	William Haade
Paddy O'Rourke	Regis Toomey
Monahan	J. M. Kerrigan
Cookie	Fuzzy Knight
Al Brett	Harry Woods
Dollarhide	Lon Chaney, Jr.
General U. S. Grant	Joseph Crehan
Mame	Julia Faye
Rose	Sheila Darcy

Also in the cast, among others: Joseph Sawyer, Earl Askam, Byron Foulger, Russell Hicks, May Beatty, Stanley Andrews, Jack Richardson, Mary MacLaren, Jane Keckley, Max Davidson, Elmo Lincoln, Lane Chandler, William Pawley, Emory Parnell, Frank Shannon, Walter Long, Monte Blue, Maude Fealy, E. J. LeSaint, Nestor Paiva, Ed Brady, Richard Denning, David Newell, Stanhope Wheatcroft, Noble Johnson, Mala.

REVIEWS

"Paramount and DeMille have a box-office winner in *Union Pacific*. It's a socko spec, sure-fire for big grosses right down the line. On its size and scope, the DeMille production is undeniable film fare."

The Weekly *Variety*,
May 3, 1939.

"In his much heralded railroad saga, *Union Pacific*, Cecil B. DeMille has again this week demonstrated on the screen his special art of the epic with an action tale on the big canvas of the American west and its romantic, dramatic tradition. Excitement is the dominant emotion, with swift succession of contrasting materials and episodes, grim and gay, often furious, sometimes funny. The narrative and action take hold at the start and never let go."

Joseph F. Coughlin in
The Motion Picture Herald,
April 29, 1939.

Akim Tamiroff and Lynne Overman

Barbara Stanwyck
and Joel McCrea

317

Joel McCrea and players

Robert Preston and Barbara Stanwyck

The Indian fight

Barbara Stanwyck

Robert Preston and Barbara Stanwyck

Joseph Crehan as Ulysses S. Grant (*In foreground*)

The Indian fight

Regis Toomey and Anthony Quinn

Anthony Quinn and Joel McCrea

George Bancroft

Preston Foster

Walter Hampden

Robert Preston,
Paulette Goddard, and Preston Foster

Paulette Goddard and Madeleine Carroll

Gary Cooper, Paulette Goddard
and Robert Preston

NORTH WEST MOUNTED POLICE

Produced and directed by Cecil B. DeMille. Original screenplay by Alan Le May, Jesse Lasky, Jr., and C. Gardner Sullivan. Cameramen: Victor Milner and W. Howard Green. Film Editor: Anne Bauchens. Music Score: Victor Young. Executive Producer: William LeBaron. Associate Producer: William H. Pine. Released by Paramount Pictures, Inc., October 22, 1940. Technicolor. Thirteen reels.

STORY

In 1885 in Canada the Riel Rebellion occurred, an uprising of half-breeds and Indians that amounted to civil war when they formed an independent Metis Nation. The North West Mounted Police acted as a body to quiet the revolt. Sgt. Jim Brett, a young Mountie, is somewhat too wedded to the military to suit the girl he loves, an Anglican nurse, April Logan. Dusty Rivers, a Texas ranger, pursues into Canada the trail of a man wanted for murder in Texas. This killer, Jacques Corbeau, is also wanted in the Northwest on a charge of murder. Both Brett and Rivers are rivals not only to bring Corbeau to justice, but also as suitors for April Logan. Corbeau's half-breed daughter Louvette entices another Mountie, April's brother, to neglect his duties, thereby leading the troopers into ambush. Dusty Rivers returns to Texas with the body of the wanted killer, while April Logan stays in Canada with Sergeant Brett.

CAST

Dusty Rivers	Gary Cooper
April Logan	Madeleine Carroll
Louvette Corbeau	Paulette Goddard
Sgt. Jim Brett	Preston Foster
Ronnie Logan	Robert Preston
Jacques Corbeau	George Bancroft
Tod McDuff	Lynne Overman
Dan Duroc	Akim Tamiroff
Big Bear	Walter Hampden
Shorty	Lon Chaney, Jr.
Inspector Cabot	Montagu Love
Louis Riel	Francis J. McDonald
Johnny Pelang	George E. Stone
Supt. Harrington	Willard Robertson
Constable Larry Moore	Regis Toomey
Constable Thornton	Richard Denning
Constable Carter	Douglas Kennedy
Constable Dumont	Robert Ryan
Constable Fenton	James Seay
Constable Fyffe	Lane Chandler
Constable Ackroyd	Ralph Byrd
Constable Kent	Eric Alden
Constable Rankin	Wallace Reid, Jr.
Constable Herrick	Bud Geary
Captain Gower	Evan Thomas
Sergeant Field	Jack Pennick
Corporal Underhill	Rod Cameron
Surgeon Roberts	Davidson Clark
Bugler	Jack Chapin
Wandering Spirit	Chief Thundercloud
The Crow	Harry Burns
Lesur	Lou Merrill
Mrs. Burns	Clara Blandick
Mrs. Shorty	Ynez Seabury
Ekawe	Eva Puig
Wapiskau	Julia Faye

Also in the cast, among others: Weldon Heyburn, Phillip Terry, George Regas, Jack Luden, Soledad Jimenez, Emory Parnell, Ed Brady, William Haade, Colin Tapley, Nestor Paiva, Donald Curtis, Jane Keckley, Noble Johnson, Monte Blue, Mala.

Gary Cooper and Paulette Goddard

REVIEWS

"Color and the screen long ago ceased to be strangers, but DeMille has lifted the visual element of his production to a new plane. Although this is his 64th personally directed feature and he has used color frequently to highlight certain passages, this is the first time he has employed the tints throughout. The results are highly gratifying."

The Weekly *Variety*,
October 23, 1940.

"All along we knew that Cecil B. DeMille and Technicolor were fated to meet; all along we expected that the result would be something to see. But barely did we anticipate anything quite as colossal to emerge from that historic conjunction as *North West Mounted Police*..."

Bosley Crowther in
The New York Times,
November 7, 1940.

"*North West Mounted Police* is a movie in the grand style—God's own biggest trees and mountains for prop and backdrop; stanch courage and lofty aims among the good people; cunning and treachery lurking within the sinister forces; the ominous note of doom finally stifled by the fortitude of noble men."

Time,
November 11, 1940.

Regis Toomey and Robert Preston

Gary Cooper and Indian players

Paulette Goddard and Robert Preston

Gary Cooper and Madeleine Carroll

Madeleine Carroll and Preston Foster

Francis McDonald, George Bancroft, and renegade players

Robert Preston and Paulette Goddard

Paulette Goddard

Madeleine Carroll, Preston Foster, and Mountie players

Ray Milland and John Wayne

Paulette Goddard
and Raymond Massey

326

John Wayne and Paulette Goddard

Paulette Goddard and Ray Milland

REAP THE WILD WIND

Directed by Cecil B. DeMille. Screenplay by Alan LeMay, Charles Bennett, and Jesse Lasky, Jr., based on the novel by Thelma Strabel. Cameramen: Victor Milner and William V. Skall. Underwater Photography: Dewey Wrigley. Film Editor: Anne Bauchens. Music Score: Victor Young. Executive Producer: Buddy G. DeSylva. Associate Producer: William H. Pine. Released by Paramount Pictures, Inc., March 19, 1942. Technicolor. Thirteen reels.

STORY

Open piracy flourishes along Key West, and salvage businesses such as the one conducted by Loxi Claiborne might have thrived if King Cutler's boats were not always first at the scene of the wreck. Loxi has reason to believe that King may actually be responsible for the wrecks. She rescues Captain Jack Stuart from drowning, falls in love with him, and takes him to Steve Tolliver to ask that he give Stuart another ship to command. Both men become rivals for Loxi's favors. There is a terrible sea wreck, in which Loxi's young cousin, Drusilla, a stowaway, loses her life. To collect evidence against the suspect, King Cutler, both Stuart and Tolliver go down to the bottom of the sea in diving suits. They are attacked by a giant squid, but Stuart frees Tolliver, who returns with the damning evidence.

327

Ray Milland, Paulette Goddard, and Lynne Overman

Charles Bickford and Ray Milland

Lynne Overman, Ray Milland, and Robert Preston

John Wayne and Ray Milland

CAST

Stephen Tolliver	Ray Milland
Captain Jack Stuart	John Wayne
Loxi Claiborne	Paulette Goddard
King Cutler	Raymond Massey
Dan Cutler	Robert Preston
Drusilla Alston	Susan Hayward
Captain Phillip Philpott	Lynne Overman
Mate of the "Tyfib"	Charles Bickford
Commodore Devereaux	Walter Hampden
Maum Maria	Louise Beavers
Mrs. Claiborne	Elisabeth Risdon
Mrs. Mottram	Janet Beecher
Aunt Henrietta Beresford	Hedda Hopper
Ivy Devereaux	Martha O'Driscoll
Widgeon	Victor Kilian
Salt Meat	Oscar Polk
Chinkapin	Ben Carter
The Lamb	William Davis
Sam	Lane Chandler
Judge Marvin	Davidson Clark
Captain of the "Pelican"	Lou Merrill
Doctor Jepson	Frank M. Thomas
Captain Carruthers	Keith Richards
Lubbock	Victor Varconi
Port Captain	J. Farrell Macdonald
Mace	Harry Woods
Master Shipwright	Raymond Hatton
Lieut. Farragut	Milburn Stone
"Claiborne" Lookout	Dave Wengren
Cadge	Tony Paton
Charleston Ladies	Barbara Britton
	Julia Faye
	Ameda Lambert
Charleston Beaux	D'Arcy Miller
	Bruce Warren

Also in the cast, among others: Forrest Taylor, George Melford, John Sainpolis, Stanhope Wheatcroft, Nestor Paiva, Ed Brady, William Haade, Frank C. Shannon, Buddy Pepper, Tom Chatterton, Frank Richards, Hayden Stevenson, Emory Parnell, Stanley Andrews, Byron Foulger, William Cabanne, Mildred Harris, Hope Landin, Claire McDowell, Dorothy Sebastian, Jack Luden, Monte Blue, Ottola Nesmith, Frank Ferguson, Max Davidson, Billy Elmer, Gertrude Astor, Maurice Costello.

Ray Milland, Paulette Goddard, and Raymond Massey

John Wayne and Paulette Goddard

Louise Beavers, Susan Hayward, and Paulette Goddard

Milburn Stone, Walter Hampden,
and Ray Milland

REVIEWS

"Cecil Blount DeMille, in celebration of his 30th anniversary in pictures, turns to a swash-buckling sea spectacle lavishly splashed in Technicolor. His production and direction of *Reap the Wild Wind*, from Thelma Strabel's *Saturday Evening Post* novel, may well be treasured as the last such lush spectacle moviegoers are likely to see until the end of the war. The show, on a grand DeMille scale, is technically magnificent and will earn many times its cost at the nation's box-offices."

The Hollywood Reporter,
March 19, 1942.

"*Reap the Wild Wind* is not by any manner of means a notable film. It never fails, though, to be an outstanding show. Since that was exactly what DeMille was intent on producing, he has every right to be very proud of his latest achievement in a long and lucrative association with the screen. It seems highly unlikely to me that the producer-director will ever be ranked with the great craftsmen of the cinema, but he has given the medium great impetus time after time, when it needed it badly."

Howard Barnes in
The New York Herald Tribune,
March 29, 1942.

Paulette Goddard, Lynne Overman,
and Susan Hayward

Gary Cooper

Laraine Day and Gary Cooper

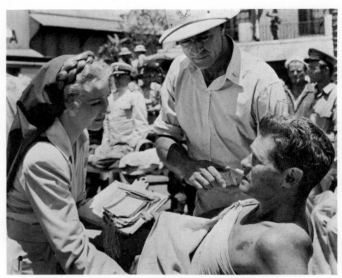

Signe Hasso, Gary Cooper, and Paul Kelly

Dennis O'Keefe and Carol Thurston

THE STORY OF DR. WASSELL

Produced and directed by Cecil B. DeMille. Screenplay by Alan LeMay, Charles Bennett, based on the story of Dr. Wassell as related by him and fifteen of the wounded sailors involved, and also on the story by James Hilton. Cameramen: Victor Milner and William Snyder. Film Editor: Anne Bauchens. Music Score: Victor Young. Executive Producer: Buddy DeSylva. Associate Producer: Sidney Bidell. Released by Paramount Pictures, Inc., April 26, 1944. Technicolor. Fifteen reels.

STORY

In the darkest days of World War II, when Japan was sweeping every victory, Dr. Corydon M. Wassell takes over the wounded men on the crippled cruiser "Marblehead," conveys them inland by train through bombings to evacuation against stern orders on the one vessel left. He runs the gauntlet of Japanese destroyers, submarines, and planes to safety in Australia. Under the eyes of Madeline, the nurse who loves him, Dr. Wassell, thinking he will at least be court-martialed, receives the Navy Cross "for especial devotion to duty and utter disregard of personal safety while in contact with enemy forces, during evacuation of the wounded by the United States Navy from Java."

CAST

Dr. Corydon M. Wassell	Gary Cooper
Madeline	Laraine Day
Bettina	Signe Hasso
Hopkins (Hoppy)	Dennis O'Keefe
Tremartini	Carol Thurston
Lieut. Dirk Van Daal	Carl Esmond
Murdock	Paul Kelly
Anderson (Andy)	Elliott Reid
Commander Bill Goggins	Stanley Ridges
Johnny	Renny McEvoy
Alabam	Oliver Thorndike
Ping	Philip Ahn
Ruth	Barbara Britton
Kraus	Joel Allen
Whaley	James Millican
Francis	Melvin Francis
Borghetti	Mike Kilian
Hunter	Doodles Weaver
Dr. Wei	Richard Loo
Dr. Holmes	Davidson Clark
Arkansas Mail Carrier	Si Jenks
Lieut. Bainbridge	Morton Lowry
Dr. Ralph Wayne	Lester Matthews
Captain Carruthers	Richard Nugent
Dr. Vranken	Ludwig Donath
Admiral	Minor Watson
Captain Ryk	Victor Varconi
Mrs. Wayne	Catherine Craig
English Mother	Edith Barrett
English Boy	Billy Severn
Captain Balan	George Macready
Admiral Hart	Edward Fielding
Captain in Charge of Evacuation	Harvey Stephens
Captain's Aide	Frank Wilcox
Rear Admiral (Australia)	Minor Watson
Rear Admiral's Aide	Edmund MacDonald
Javanese Temple Guide	Frank Puglia

Also in the cast, among others: Ottola Nesmith, Irving Bacon, Hugh Beaumont, Edward Earle, Jody Gilbert, Anthony Caruso, Bruce Warren, Louis Jean Heydt, George Lynn, Fred Kohler, Jr., Louis Borell, Frank Mayo, Gavin Muir, Ivan Triesault, Gordon Richards, Ann Doran, Lane Chandler, Boyd Irwin, John Meredith, Mildred Harris, Greta Granstedt, Carlyle Blackwell, William Forrest, Elmo Lincoln.

Carl Esmond and Signe Hasso

Gary Cooper

Frank Puglia and Gary Cooper

REVIEWS

"It actually happened—that is the point! Even with the elaborate trimmings of a Cecil DeMille production, we never lose sight of the fact that the heroics are real. It is this particular point that gives heart and stability to a picture that, at times, seems almost too ornate for the saga of a great doctor who refused to abandon fifteen desperately injured seamen of Uncle Sam's Navy and literally went through hell to bring them back home."

Louella O. Parsons in
The Los Angeles Examiner, June 8, 1944.

"Because this is the factual story of Dr. Wassell's heroic evacuation of twelve men, plus himself, from Java in earlier stages of the war, it packs more interest than otherwise might have been the case. The exploits of the by-now famed Naval Commander have been brought to the screen on a lavish scale by Cecil B. DeMille, with an exceptionally fine cast and good comedy relief. The entertainment value, even had the scenario been fictional, is very strong. Production excellence and good color photography are added assets. Gross possibilities are exceptionally favorable despite any trend away from so-called war pictures."

The Weekly *Variety*,
April 4, 1944.

"I do not feel I need to have been there to know that his story is one of the great ones of this war; also, that it could be much better told through moving pictures than by any other means; also that on both counts Cecil DeMille's screen version of it is to be regretted beyond qualification. It whips the story, in every foot, into a nacreous foam of lies whose speciousness is only the more painful because Mr. DeMille is so obviously free from any desire to alter the truth except for what he considers to be its own advantage. All the more touching, and terrifying, is the fact that Dr. Wassell himself thinks that the picture, with a few trifling exceptions, is true and good."

James Agee in
The Nation,
June 10, 1944.

Gary Cooper, Dennis O'Keefe, and soldiers

Gary Cooper and Si Jenkins

334

Gary Cooper and Paul Kelly

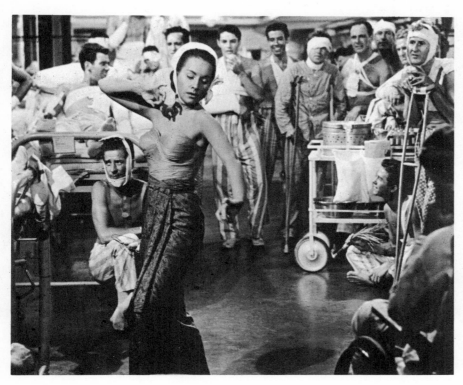

Carol Thurston

335

Gary Cooper

Virginia Grey and Gary Cooper

Virginia Campbell and Gary Cooper

Paulette Goddard and Gary Cooper

UNCONQUERED

Produced and directed by Cecil B. DeMille. Screenplay by Charles Bennett, Fredric M. Frank, and Jesse Lasky, Jr., based on the novel by Neil H. Swanson. Cameraman: Ray Rennahan. Film Editor: Anne Bauchens. Music Score: Victor Young. Released by Paramount Pictures, Inc., September 24, 1947. Technicolor, 35mm. 147 minutes.

STORY

Abby Hale, a pretty English convict girl, is ordered deported as a potential slave to the American Colonies. Captain Holden saves her from being auctioned into slavery, and when she is captured by Indians and subjected to a slow tortuous death, Captain Holden appears in a flash of gunpowder smoke, convincing the Indians that he is a god, so that they relinquish Abby to him. Abby is also pursued by Martin Garth, a villain engaged in selling illegal firearms to Indians. Captain Holden risks court-martial in exposing Garth as prodding Indians into massacring the white colonists, and Holden is able to lead a small band of men to the defense of Fort Pitt, fooling the attacking savages just when the beleaguered occupants of the Fort are about to surrender. Abby and Holden find peace and happiness finally when all the villains who pursue them are killed off.

Gary Cooper and Mike Mazurki

CAST

Captain Christopher Holden	Gary Cooper
Abby Hale	Paulette Goddard
Martin Garth	Howard Da Silva
Guyasuta, Chief of the Senecas	Boris Karloff
Jeremy Love	Cecil Kellaway
John Fraser	Ward Bond
Hannah	Katherine DeMille
Captain Steele	Henry Wilcoxon
Lord Chief Justice	Sir C. Aubrey Smith
Captain Simeon Ecuyer	Victor Varconi
Diana	Virginia Grey
Leach	Porter Hall
Dave Bone	Mike Mazurki
Colonel George Washington	Richard Gaines
Mrs. John Fraser	Virginia Campbell
Lieut. Fergus McKenzie	Gavin Muir
Sir William Johnson	Alan Napier
Mrs. Pratt	Nan Sunderland
Sioto, Medicine Man	Marc Lawrence
Evelyn	Jane Nigh

Also in the cast, among others: Robert Warwick, Lloyd Bridges, Oliver Thorndike, Frank Wilcox, Raymond Hatton, Julia Faye, Clarence Muse, Boyd Irwin, Hope Landin, Richard Reeves, Noble Johnson, James Horne, Ottola Nesmith, Fred Kohler, Jr., Greta Granstedt, William Haade, Jeff Corey, Mike Kilian, Lane Chandler, John Miljan, Francis Ford, Francis J. McDonald.

Gavin Muir (left) and Gary Cooper

Paulette Goddard and Howard Da Silva

Paulette Goddard, Virginia Campbell, and Gary Cooper

Marc Lawrence and Paulette Goddard

REVIEWS

"Like David O. Selznick's *Duel in the Sun*, this one is so un-DeMille it's surprising. But, like *Duel*, it will get business. As a spec it has sufficient size and scope to command plenty of b.o. . . . Despite the ten-twent-thirt meller-dramatics and the frequently inept script, the performances are convincing, a great tribute to the cast because that dialogue and those situations try the best of troupers."

The Daily *Variety*,
September 24, 1947.

"Spectacularly, stirringly and with full panoply of gaudy color, Cecil B. DeMille again screen-vitalizes a chapter out of American history in his picture *Unconquered*. One may also say that he has supplied both a boisterous and sensational delineation of the frontiersman's era with the full complement of DeMille devices, even to the famous bath sequence, a dip into the serial thrillers when the hero and heroine shoot the rapids to the edge of a waterfall, and the staging of the battle of Fort Pitt that far outdoes any conflict that was ever dreamt up for a world's fair carnival."

Edwin Schallert in
The Los Angeles Times,
November 26, 1947.

"Just about as subtle as a juvenile comic strip and cut on a comparable pattern, so far as episode and action are concerned, it tells a tempestuous story of a doughty frontiersman's escapades among the British redcoats and the redskins in the pre-Revolutionary wilds. . . and it is also deplorably evident that *Unconquered*, in this year of grace, is as viciously anti-redskin as *The Birth of a Nation* was anti-Negro long years back."

Bosley Crowther in
The New York Times,
October 19, 1947.

"*The Unconquered* is Cecil Blount DeMille's florid, $5,000,000 Technicolored celebration of Gary Cooper's virility, Paulette Goddard's femininity and the American Frontier Spirit. The movie is getting such stentorian ballyhoo that a lot of cinemagoers are likely to think less of it than it deserves. It is, to be sure, a huge, high-colored chunk of hokum; but the most old-fashioned thing about it is its exuberance, a quality which 66-year-old Director DeMille preserves almost single-handed from the old days when even the people who laughed at movies couldn't help liking them."

James Agee in
Time,
October 27, 1947.

Gavin Muir and Gary Cooper

SAMSON AND DELILAH

Produced and directed by Cecil B. DeMille. Screenplay by Jesse L. Lasky, Jr., Fredric M. Frank, based on a treatment by Harold Lamb of the story of Samson and Delilah in the Holy Bible, Judges 13-16 and Vladimir Jabotinsky's novel, Judge and Fool. Cameraman: George Barnes. Film Editor: Anne Bauchens. Music Score: Victor Young. Released by Paramount Pictures, Inc., October 21, 1949. Technicolor, 35mm. 131 minutes.

STORY

Samson, the strong Danite, seeks the hand in marriage of Semadar of the Philistines, but she is killed in the fight that ensues when her people revile Samson. Her younger sister, Delilah, out of revenge, determines to learn the secret of Samson's strength, and so destroy him. He becomes infatuated with her, and confides that the secret of his strength lies in his unshorn

hair. During a drunken slumber, Samson is
shorn of his locks by Delilah, who then delivers
him to his enemies, the Philistines, on condition
that they neither touch his flesh nor slay him.
Cunningly, they blind him and make a lowly
slave of him. His strength returns as his hair
grows, and on the day he is brought into the
temple to be ridiculed, Samson brings everything
down in ruins by pushing the two main pillars
aside, destroying along with everybody else both
Delilah and himself.

Victor Mature

Victor Mature, William Farnum, and Angela Lansbury

CAST

Samson	Victor Mature
Delilah	Hedy Lamarr
The Saran of Gaza	George Sanders
Semadar	Angela Lansbury
Ahtur	Henry Wilcoxon
Miriam	Olive Deering
Hazeleponit	Fay Holden
Hisham	Julia Faye
Saul	Russell Tamblyn
Tubal	William Farnum
Teresh	Lane Chandler
Targil	Moroni Olsen
Story Teller	Francis J. McDonald
Garmiskar	William Davis
Lesh Lakish	John Miljan
Fat Philistine Merchant	Arthur Q. Bryan
Spectator	Laura Elliot
Lord of Ashdod	Victor Varconi
Lord of Gath	John Parrish
Lord of Ekron	Frank Wilcox
Lord of Ashkelon	Russell Hicks
First Priest	Boyd Davis
Lord Sharif	Fritz Leiber
Leader of Philistine Soldiers	Mike Mazurki
Merchant Prince	Davidson Clark
Wounded Messenger	George Reeves
Bar Simon	Pedro de Cordoba
Village Barber	Frank Reicher
Prince	Colin Tapley

Also in the cast, among others: Nils Asther,
Frank Mayo, George Zoritch, Crauford Kent,
Charles Meredith, Pierre Watkin, Robert St.
Angelo, Charles Judels, Wheaton Chambers,
Fred Kohler, Jr., Tom Tyler, Paul Scardon,
Gordon Richards, Edward Peil, James Horne,
Philo McCullough, Ottola Nesmith, Ynez Sea-
bury, Claire DuBrey, Greta Granstedt, Karen
Morley.

Victor Mature

Hedy Lamarr, Victor Mature, and George Sanders

Victor Mature and Hedy Lamarr

Hedy Lamarr and Victor Mature

Victor Mature

Lane Chandler, Harry Woods, Ed Hinton, Hedy
Lamarr, Moroni Olsen, and Steve Roberts

REVIEWS

"It's a fantastic picture for this era in its size, in its lavishness, in the corniness of its storytelling and in its old-fashioned technique. But it adds up to first-class entertainment. The smarties and the hinterlanders will view it from diametrically opposed standpoints, but whether laughing at it or with it, neither the hepsters nor the squares will find any of its two hours and eight minutes dull or unenjoyable. And as for the

kids, Samson is the greatest invention since Superman . . . . DeMille's direction is broad and sweeping, reminiscent in technique of his successes of as long as 30 years ago, yet in keeping with the pic quality of the subject."

The Weekly *Variety*,
October 26, 1949.

"It may be said of Cecil B. DeMille that since 1913, when he teamed up with Jesse Lasky to

Hedy Lamarr, George Sanders, and Olive Deering

Hedy Lamarr and George Sanders

Julia Faye, Victor Mature, and Hedy Lamarr

create *The Squaw Man*, he has never taken a step backward. He has never taken a step forward, either, but somehow he has managed to survive in a chancy industry where practically everybody is incessantly going up, down, or sideways, and ordinarily only the dead are absolutely still. Perhaps DeMille's survival is due to the fact that he decided in his movie nonage to ally himself with God as his co-maker and to get his major scripts from the Bible; which he has always handled with the proprietary air of a gentleman fondling old love letters. In *Samson and Delilah*, DeMille is back on his usual beat, but this time I'm not at all sure that he has produced a work that enhances the glory of him or his Associate."

The New Yorker,
December 31, 1949.

Victor Mature and Hedy Lamarr

"Cecil B. DeMille returns to the Book with the greatest circulation of them all and from this, the Bible, which has furnished him ideas for several of his greatest successes, he now finds another: the story of Samson and Delilah. If DeMille can outdo DeMille, this time it has been done. For in *Samson and Delilah* he has come up with a king-size attraction which showmen everywhere will long have cause to remember."

"Red Kann" in
The Motion Picture Herald,
October 22, 1949.

"The first thing to be said about it, before the echoes have even died, is that, if ever there was a movie for DeMillions, here it is. For Mr. DeMille, that veteran genie who has already engineered three quasi-religious film pageants that tower in the annals of the screen, has here led his carpenters and actors and costumers and camera crews into the vast manufacture of a spectacle that out-Babels anything he's done. There are more flowing garments in this picture, more chariots, more temples, more peacock

Victor Mature, Henry Wilcoxon, and Hedy Lamarr

plumes, more animals, more pillows, more spear-carriers, more beards, and more sex than ever before. At least, that's the sizable impression which Mr. DeMille has achieved by bringing together the Old Testament and Technicolor for the first time."

Bosley Crowther in
The New York Times,
December 22, 1949.

Victor Mature

Hedy Lamarr and Victor Mature

Hedy Lamarr and Victor Mature

"*Samson and Delilah* bedizens the Biblical story with all that $3,000,000 can buy: Hedy Lamarr, Victor Mature, 600 extras and eye-crashing Technicolor, mixed by the lavish, lily-gilding hand of Cecil B. DeMille. The result may not be quite Old Testament, but it is Bible story shrewdly blended with sex, spectacle, and the merest suggestion of social comment to keep it abreast of current Hollywood trends. It is unlikely to tarnish Producer-Director DeMille's reputation for consistently making (as well as spending) more money on pictures than anybody else.... DeMille has provided plenty of gorgeous scenery for all the actors to chew on, and has filmed his spectacular scenes with technical virtuosity and boundless gusto. Even lovers of cinematic art who recognize *Samson and Delilah* as a run-of-DeMille epic should enjoy it as a simple-minded spree. In its way, it is as much fun as a robust, well-organized circus."

Time,
December 26, 1949.

Victor Mature

Charlton Heston and Gloria Grahame

Dorothy Lamour

THE GREATEST SHOW ON EARTH

Produced and directed by Cecil B. DeMille. Screenplay by Fredric M. Frank, Barre Lyndon, and Theodore St. John, from a story by Fredric M. Frank and Frank Cavett. Cameramen: George Barnes, J. Peverell Marley, Wallace Kelley. Film Editor: Anne Bauchens. Music Score: Victor Young. Associate Producer: Henry Wilcoxon. Produced with the cooperation of Ringling Brothers-Barnum & Bailey Circus. Released by Paramount Pictures, Inc., January 2, 1952. Technicolor, 35mm. 153 minutes.

STORY

Holly, queen flyer of the circus, is in love with Brad, the circus manager, but his whole life is the circus. He imports a top aerialist, Sebastian, and gives the center ring to him instead of to Holly, who quarrels with Brad, but is intrigued by Sebastian, with whom she competes dangerously for top honors in performing hazardous tricks. Angel, the elephant girl, also has a yen

351

Ringling Bros.-Barnum & Bailey aerial acts

for Brad, but her boss, Klaus, is jealous and when Brad fires him, Klaus rigs a robbing of the circus train, which is spectacularly wrecked. Klaus is killed and Brad injured. Buttons, a clown, is actually a doctor wanted for murder, and when he saves Brad's life and patches up Sebastian's arm damaged in a trapeze fall, Buttons is forced to reveal his identity and is taken into custody by the FBI. Sebastian finds happiness with Angel, and the show goes on.

CAST

Holly	Betty Hutton
Sebastian	Cornel Wilde
Brad	Charlton Heston
Phyllis	Dorothy Lamour
Angel	Gloria Grahame
Buttons	James Stewart
Klaus	Lyle Bettger
FBI Man	Henry Wilcoxon
Henderson	Lawrence Tierney
Emmet Kelly	Himself
Cucciola	Himself
Antoinette Concello	Herself
John Ringling North	Himself
Harry	John Kellogg
Jack Steelman	John Ridgely
Circus Doctor	Frank Wilcox
Ringmaster	Bob Carson
Buttons' Mother	Lillian Albertson
Violet	Julia Faye

Also in the cast, among others: Top Circus Acts of the World, Gloria Drew, Noel Neill, John Crawford, Keith Richards, Dolores Hall, Robert St. Angelo, Lane Chandler, Davidson Clark, Dorothy Adams, Fred Kohler, Jr., Greta Granstedt, Ottola Nesmith, David Newell, Josephine Whitell, Bess Flowers, Stanley Andrews, Queenie Smith, Kathleen Freeman, Ross Bagdasarian, and guest appearances by Bing Crosby and Bob Hope.

REVIEWS

"He [DeMille] is obviously enraptured by all the tinselled glamour, awed by the feats of daring, impressed by the sense of danger that lurks everywhere in circus life. And all of this he has captured with his unrivaled sense of what will make a good movie. Here he doesn't have to pretend an historical accuracy or assume a reli-

Betty Hutton

gious sententiousness. Here, against the background of a circus, all the faults that caused such critical mutterings about *Samson and Delilah* are converted into positive virtues. Here it's right for DeMille to be vulgar, obvious, gaudy. For what else is a circus? In this film any other approach would produce the same pretentiousness that vitiated his earlier epics."

Saturday Review,
January 12, 1952.

"*The Greatest Show on Earth* is as apt a handle for Cecil B. DeMille's Technicolored version of the Ringling Bros.–Barnum & Bailey Circus as it is for the sawdust extravaganza itself. This is the circus with more entertainment, more thrills, more spangles and as much Big Top atmosphere as RB–B&B itself can offer. It's a smash certainly for high-wire grosses."

The Weekly *Variety,*
January 2, 1952.

"In *The Greatest Show on Earth,* Cecil B. DeMille attempts to do for the Ringling Brothers and Barnum & Bailey what he did for God and Moses in *The Ten Commandments.* Mr. DeMille, who occasionally takes part in the film as an off-screen commentator, makes it clear from the

Betty Hutton and James Stewart

Cornel Wilde and Betty Hutton

opening frame that the circus created by the Brothers and B. & B. is an awesome affair, and for a while it seems as though the Master is going to do a straight documentary on the subject, to the chagrin of his expensive cast. But presently he gets out of the way and lets the performers go into action."

The New Yorker,
January 19, 1952.

"Within his established province of theatrical spectacle, Mr. DeMille has at last achieved a merger of the spectacular with the real. Even the romantic story which he had written for the film—a rambling criss-cross of complications in several circus people's lives—is reflective of the daily romance of circus reality . . . . In short, the circus, an actuality, presented Mr. DeMille with a subject that challenged even his skill at representing dazzle on the screen—and he handled it in superior fashion. Indeed, looking back on his career, this film glorification of the circus would appear that one, far-off, divine event to which the whole creation of Cecil B. DeMille supremely moved."

Bosley Crowther in
The New York Times,
January 20, 1952.

Gloria Grahame

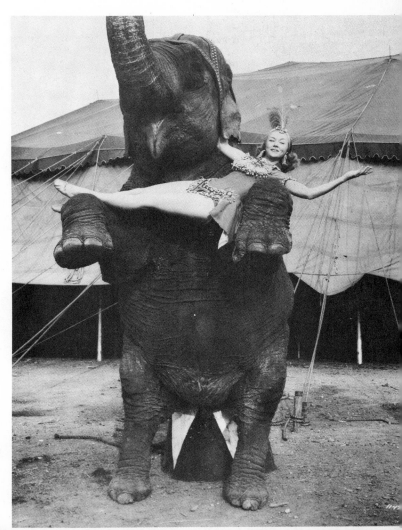

"If art were merely a matter of fitting form to content, the movie would be a masterpiece, for DeMille and the circus are fated for each other. By sprinkling his footage with shots of circus audiences munching all the tidbits of the refreshment stand, DeMille tightens his claim to another distinction: *Greatest Show* is likely to sell more popcorn than any movie ever made."

Time,
January 14, 1952.

"Mr. DeMille is so accomplished a showman that one is astonished he did not just photograph a circus performance without the synthetic story he injected here. After all, the Ringling Brothers–Barnum and Bailey Circus is a wonder in itself. There are millions in this country, and more millions throughout the world, who have never seen it. DeMille's directorial ability is sufficiently skillful for him to have put the circus on the screen with even intensified tempo. But he had to add love interest—and schmaltz it all up."

Films in Review,
February, 1952.

James Stewart, Betty Hutton,
and Charlton Heston

Betty Hutton, James Stewart, and cast

354

Cornel Wilde and Betty Hutton

Dorothy Lamour, Betty Hutton, and players

Betty Hutton and Charlton Heston

Gloria Grahame
and Lyle Bettger

355

Charlton Heston, John Derek, Debra Paget, Yvonne De Carlo, and Nina Foch

Debra Paget and John Derek

THE TEN COMMANDMENTS

Produced and directed by Cecil B. DeMille. Screenplay by Aeneas MacKenzie, Jesse L. Lasky, Jr., Jack Gariss, and Fredric M. Frank, from Dorothy Clarke Wilson's novel Prince of Egypt, *Rev. J. H. Ingraham's novel* Pillar of Fire, *and Rev. G. E. Southon's* On Eagle's Wings, *in accordance with the ancient texts of Josephus, Eusebius, Philo,* The Midrash, *and* The Holy Scriptures. *Cameraman: Loyal Griggs. Additional Photography: J. Peverell Marley, John Warren, Wallace Kelley. Film Editor: Anne Bauchens. Music Score: Elmer Bernstein. Released by Paramount Pictures Inc., October 5, 1956. Vistavision Technicolor, 35mm. 221 minutes.*

STORY

When Rameses I is told that a Deliverer is to be born who will set free the enslaved children of Israel, he condemns all newborn male Hebrew children to death. But one mother, Yochabel,

357

places her newborn, Moses, in a crude cradle of bulrushes and sets it afloat upon the Nile. The daughter of Pharaoh, Bithiah, finds the baby Moses, and adopts him, and unwittingly brings in the real mother and sister to bring him up. Moses grows to maturity as a Prince of Egypt, and is desired by the seductive princess Nefretiri. But Moses kills an Egyptian who smites a Hebrew, and his true past is disclosed. Moses is exiled into the desert, where he marries Sephora, eldest daughter of Jethro. God appears to Moses in a burning bush, commanding him to set free from bondage the Children of Israel. Moses confronts the new Pharaoh, calling down plagues from heaven until Pharaoh relents and lets Moses lead the slaves to freedom; but then Pharaoh repents of his decision and gives chase to the Israelites, only to be drowned with all his hosts in the Red Sea after the Children of Israel have passed across safely when Jehovah parted the waters. Moses goes onto the Holy Mountain, Sinai, and in his absence his people abandon their one God and worship the pagan Golden Calf. Moses receives the Ten Commandments, destroys the Golden Calf and the idolaters, leads his people for forty years to the slopes of Mount Nibo on the River Jordan, and then goes up alone onto the mountain to face and be received by his God.

Charlton Heston and Yul Brynner

Edward G. Robinson

359

Martha Scott

Judith Anderson and Nina Foch

Charlton Heston, Yul Brynner, Sir Cedric Hardwicke,
and Anne Baxter

CAST

Moses	Charlton Heston
Rameses	Yul Brynner
Nefretiri	Anne Baxter
Dathan	Edward G. Robinson
Sephora	Yvonne De Carlo
Lilia	Debra Paget
Joshua	John Derek
Sethi	Sir Cedric Hardwicke
Bithiah	Nina Foch
Yochabel	Martha Scott
Memnet	Judith Anderson
Baka	Vincent Price
Aaron	John Carradine
Jethro	Eduard Franz
Miriam	Olive Deering
Mered	Donald Curtis
Jannes	Douglass Dumbrille
Abiram	Frank DeKova
Amminadab	H. B. Warner
Pentaur	Henry Wilcoxon
Hur Ben Caleb	Lawrence Dobkin
Elisheba	Julia Faye
Jethro's Daughters	Lisa Mitchell
	Joanna Merlin
	Joyce Vanderveen
	Noelle Williams
	Pat Richard
	Diane Hall

Yul Brynner

Rameses' Charioteer	Abbas El Boughdadly
The Infant Moses	Fraser Heston
Gershom	Tommy Duran
Rameses' Son	Eugene Mazzola
Rameses I	Ian Keith
Korah	Ramsay Hill
The Blind One	John Miljan
Simon	Francis J. McDonald
Eleazar	Paul De Rolf
Korah's Wife	Joan Woodbury
King of Ethiopia	Woodrow Strode
Princess Tharbis	Esther Brown
Commander of the Hosts	Henry Brandon
Amalekite Herder	Touch Connors
Sardinian Captain	Clint Walker

Also in the cast, among others: Dorothy Adams, Edna Mae Cooper, Kem Dibbs, Maude Fealy, Fred Kohler, Jr., George Melford, Dorothy Neumann, Addison Richards, Keith Richards, Onslow Stevens, Frank Wilcox, Jeane Wood, Luis Alberni, Lillian Albertson, Michael Ansara, Joel Ashley, George Baxter, Robert Bice, Peter Coe, Frankie Darro, J. Stevan Darrell, Edward Earle, Antony Eustrel, Matty Fain, Franklyn Farnum, Tony George, Gavin Gordon, Kay Hammond, Peter Hansen, Walter Woolf King, Barry Macollum, Adeline de Walt Reynolds, Irene Tedrow, Robert Vaughn.

Yul Brynner, Nina Foch, and Charlton Heston

John Derek and Charlton Heston

REVIEWS

"It is appropriate that in this, the Year of the Big Picture, the second of Cecil B. DeMille's *The Ten Commandments* should appear on the screen. It has been 33 years since the first one, and doubtless there are many people who know nothing of that colossus of the old colossals except what they have read or heard. Viewing his current three-and-a-half hour work, they may find a DeMille production a trying experience now and then, but a very educational one. They are bound to be, as their parents and grandparents were, impressed."

Newsweek,
November 5, 1956.

"Religion is the most personal of human experiences. Because of that, few dramatists have succeeded in letting their spiritual beliefs pervade the materialistic fabric of words, the

Charlton Heston

Charlton Heston and Yvonne DeCarlo

Sir Cedric Hardwicke, Henry Wilcoxon, Yul Brynner, and Charlton Heston

light and shade of canvas and plaster sets, and the cold eye of the cinematograph lens. Cecil B. DeMille not only moulds religion into a set pattern of Hollywood conventions; he has also become a specialist in making entertainment of it."

Gordon Gow in
Films and Filming,
January, 1956.

"And the result of all these stupendous efforts? Something roughly comparable to an eight-foot chorus girl—pretty well put together, but much too big and much too flashy. And sometimes DeMille is worse than merely flashy. It is difficult to find another instance in which so large a golden calf has been set up without objection from religious leaders. With insuperable piety, Cinemogul DeMille claims that he has tried 'to translate the Bible back to its original form,' the form in which it was lived. Yet what he has really done is to throw sex and sand into

Charlton Heston, Sir Cedric Hardwicke,
Yul Brynner, and Anne Baxter

363

the movie-goers' eyes for almost twice as long as anybody else has ever dared to."

Time,
November 12, 1956.

"No critical appraisal can be pure rave. While DeMille has broken new ground in terms of size, he has remained conventional with the motion picture as an art form. Emphasis on physical dimension has rendered neither awesome nor profound the story of Moses. The eyes of the onlooker are filled with spectacle. Emotional tug is sometimes lacking."

The Weekly *Variety,*
October 10, 1956.

364

Yul Brynner and Charlton Heston

The Legionnaire and the Lady (Morocco) — DeMille, Marlene Dietrich, and Clark Gable

Dangerous — Don Ameche, Madeleine Carroll, and DeMille

Stella Dallas — Anne Shirley, John Boles, Barbara Stanwyck, and DeMille

"LUX PRESENTS HOLLYWOOD..."

From June 1, 1936 until January 22, 1945, Cecil B. DeMille was host and director for the "Lux Radio Theatre," one of the biggest and most popular weekly shows in the history of radio. It began in New York City, where it enjoyed a high prestige rating under the direction of Antony Stanford, who preferred to use big Broadway names in radio versions of famous Broadway plays.

In 1936 when the show was moved by its sponsor, Lever Brothers, to be aired by the Columbia Broadcasting System from Hollywood, the format was changed to become radio versions of famous film features, sometimes with the same cast as had appeared in the movie, but more often with different stars in the leading roles. This provided for, at times, some out-of-the-ordinary casting.

With DeMille at the helm, "Lux Radio Theatre" often attracted an estimated Monday night audience of forty million listeners, and by 1945 the program was netting DeMille himself an annual salary of nearly $100,000. He produced, hosted, and directed nearly all the shows presented, although an occasional guest director officiated under DeMille's supervision.

Regretfully, he terminated his position as director for the "Lux Radio Theatre" because of his refusal to pay the sum of one dollar, as approved by the Los Angeles local board of directors for AFRA (American Federation of Radio Artists) for the purpose of accumulating a fund to oppose Proposition 12 in the California November general elections. Proposition 12 would abolish the closed shop in California and would give to every Californian, regardless of affiliation or not with any union, the right to obtain and hold any job. AFRA, being a closed shop, required payment of the one-dollar assessment by all its members on or before September 1, 1944, and if that dollar was not paid, it would automatically mean suspension, prohibiting him from any radio work.

DeMille was for, and voted for, Proposition 12; he adamantly refused to pay the assessed dollar on the grounds that payment of it would cancel his vote and, furthermore, he did not believe that any union or organization had the right to levy a compulsory political assessment upon any member. Nor would he permit any other person or organization, including Lever Brothers, to pay the dollar for him.

That stand ultimately meant he could no longer work as director for "Lux Radio Theatre," and Lever Brothers subsequently spent nearly a year deciding on an adequate permanent replacement for him, eventually signing director William Keighley for the job.

The "Lux Radio Theatre" continued until June 7, 1955, but DeMille could never work again on radio, and when AFRA became AFTRA (American Federation of Television and Radio Artists), the ban still held against him, so he could never work in television either. Had he paid the dollar, he would probably have continued as Lux's director for the final ten years of its existence; by refusing to pay it, he undoubtedly turned down at least a million dollars.

It was indicative of DeMille's strong personality that he could relinquish a job he liked and which netted him almost $100,000 a year simply because of his refusal to pay one dollar in support of something to which he was opposed. When he believed he was right, he stood one hundred per cent on his belief.

The following is a list of the hour-long shows he weekly directed and supervised for "Lux Radio Theatre," along with the stars he cast in the leading roles. His personal preferences for the work of certain performers is to be noted, as

Tonight or Never — DeMille, Jeanette MacDonald, Mary Garden, and Melvyn Douglas

well as his casting of certain players in roles they would otherwise never have had a chance to interpret.

Among feminine stars, Barbara Stanwyck worked more often on the "Lux Radio Theatre" under DeMille's direction than any other actress, playing leads in fifteen different attractions. Claudette Colbert and Loretta Young tie for second place, each having played fourteen times for DeMille.

Among actors cast in leads for the Lux DeMille-directed radio plays, Don Ameche worked more often than any other male star, playing leads in eighteen different radio plays. Fred MacMurray stands next, with seventeen radio appearances for DeMille.

Some extraordinary bits of casting are immediately evidenced: Miss Stanwyck in *Wuthering Heights*, *Morning Glory*, and *Smilin' Through*; Joan Crawford in *Anna Christie*, *A Doll's House*, and *Mary of Scotland*; Don Ameche and Jean Arthur in *Seventh Heaven*; Ronald Coleman and Ida Lupino in *Rebecca*; Mickey Rooney and Judy Garland in *Merton of the Movies*—these are only a few of many. The supporting casts were always distinguished, and each show had an olio in which some outstanding personality, such as Jesse L. Lasky, Daniel Frohman, Mary Garden, or even Theda Bara, was presented to the listening audience.

Another Language— DeMille, Fred MacMurray, Bette Davis, May Robson, and John Beal

Anna Christie — Marjorie Rambeau, George Marion, Joan Crawford, and DeMille

369

Date	Title	Cast	Date	Title	Cast
June 1, 1936	*The Legionnaire and the Lady (Morocco)*	Marlene Dietrich Clark Gable	Jan. 18, 1937	*The Criminal Code*	Edward G. Robinson Beverly Roberts
June 8, 1936	*The Thin Man*	William Powell Myrna Loy	Jan. 25, 1937	*Tonight or Never*	Jeanette MacDonald Melvyn Douglas
June 15, 1936	*Burlesque*	Al Jolson Ruby Keeler	Feb. 1, 1937	*Mr. Deeds Goes to Town*	Gary Cooper Jean Arthur
June 22, 1936	*The Dark Angel*	Merle Oberon Herbert Marshall	Feb. 8, 1937	*Graustark*	Gene Raymond Anna Sten
June 29, 1936	*Irene*	Jeanette MacDonald	Feb. 15, 1937	*Brewster's Millions*	Jack Benny Mary Livingstone
July 6, 1936	*The Voice of Bugle Ann*	Lionel Barrymore Anne Shirley	Feb. 22, 1937	*Captain Blood*	Errol Flynn Olivia deHavilland
July 13, 1936	*The Brat*	Marion Davies Joel McCrea	March 1, 1937	*Cappy Ricks*	Charles Winninger Sally Eilers Richard Arlen
July 20, 1936	*The Barker*	Claudette Colbert Walter Huston Norman Foster	March 8, 1937	*Madame Butterfly*	Grace Moore Cary Grant
July 27, 1936	*Chained*	Joan Crawford Franchot Tone	March 15, 1937	*Desire*	Marlene Dietrich Herbert Marshall
August 3, 1936	*Main Street*	Barbara Stanwyck Fred MacMurray	March 22, 1937	*Death Takes a Holiday*	Fredric March Florence Eldridge
August 10, 1936	*The Jazz Singer*	Al Jolson Karen Morley	March 29, 1937	*Dulcy*	George Burns Gracie Allen
August 17, 1936	*The Vagabond King*	John Boles Evelyn Venable	April 5, 1937	*A Farewell to Arms*	Clark Gable Josephine Hutchinson
August 24, 1936	*One Sunday Afternoon*	Jack Oakie Helen Twelvetrees	April 12, 1937	*Dodsworth*	Walter Huston Nan Sunderland
August 31, 1936	*Cheating Cheaters*	George Raft June Lang	April 19, 1937	*Alibi Ike*	Joe E. Brown
Sept. 7, 1936	*Is Zat So*	James Cagney Boots Mallory	April 26, 1937	*Magnificent Obsession*	Robert Taylor Irene Dunne
Sept. 14, 1936	*Quality Street*	Brian Aherne Ruth Chatterton	May 3, 1937	*Hands Across the Table*	Claudette Colbert Joel McCrea
Sept. 21, 1936	*Trilby*	Grace Moore Peter Lorre Ralph Forbes	May 10, 1937	*Mary of Scotland*	Joan Crawford Franchot Tone
Sept. 28, 1936	*The Plutocrat*	Wallace Beery Cecelia Parker	May 17, 1937	*Another Language*	Bette Davis Fred MacMurray
Oct. 5, 1936	*Elmer the Great*	Joe E. Brown June Travis	May 24, 1937	*Under Two Flags*	Herbert Marshall Olivia deHavilland Lupe Velez
Oct. 12, 1936	*The Curtain Rises*	Ginger Rogers Warren William	May 31, 1937	*The Plainsman*	Fredric March Jean Arthur
Oct. 19, 1936	*Captain Applejack*	Frank Morgan Maureen O'Sullivan	June 7, 1937	*British Agent*	Errol Flynn Frances Farmer
Oct. 26, 1936	*Saturday's Children*	Robert Taylor Olivia deHavilland	June 14, 1937	*Madame X*	Ann Harding James Stewart
Nov. 2, 1936	*The Virginian*	Gary Cooper Helen Mack	June 21, 1937	*Monsieur Beaucaire*	Leslie Howard Elissa Landi
Nov. 9, 1936	*Alias Jimmy Valentine*	Pat O'Brien Madge Evans	June 28, 1937	*The Front Page*	Walter Winchell Josephine Hutchinson James Gleason
Nov. 16, 1936	*Conversation Piece*	Lily Pons Adolphe Menjou	July 5, 1937	*Beau Brummel*	Robert Montgomery Madge Evans
Nov. 23, 1936	*The Story of Louis Pasteur*	Paul Muni Fritz Leiber	Sept. 13, 1937	*A Star Is Born*	Janet Gaynor Robert Montgomery
Nov. 30, 1936	*Polly of the Circus*	Loretta Young James Gleason	Sept. 20, 1937	*The Outsider*	Fredric March Florence Eldridge
Dec. 7, 1936	*The Grand Duchess and the Waiter*	Robert Montgomery Elissa Landi	Sept. 27, 1937	*Cimarron*	Clark Gable Virginia Bruce
Dec. 14, 1936	*Madame Sans-Gêne*	Jean Harlow Robert Taylor	Oct. 4, 1937	*Dodsworth*	Walter Huston Nan Sunderland
Dec. 21, 1936	*The Gold Diggers*	Joan Blondell Dick Powell	Oct. 11, 1937	*Stella Dallas*	Barbara Stanwyck John Boles Anne Shirley
Dec. 28, 1936	*Cavalcade*	Herbert Marshall Madeleine Carroll	Oct. 18, 1937	*Up Pops the Devil*	Fred MacMurray Madge Evans
Jan. 4, 1937	*Men in White*	Spencer Tracy Virginia Bruce Frances Farmer	Oct. 25, 1937	*Arrowsmith*	Spencer Tracy Fay Wray
Jan. 11, 1937	*The Gilded Lily*	Claudette Colbert Fred MacMurray	Nov. 1, 1937	*A Free Soul*	Ginger Rogers Don Ameche

Nov. 8, 1937	*She Loves Me Not*	Bing Crosby Joan Blondell	
Nov. 15, 1937	*Come and Get It*	Edward Arnold Anne Shirley	
Nov. 22, 1937	*The Petrified Forest*	Herbert Marshall Margaret Sullavan	
Nov. 29, 1937	*Peg O' My Heart*	Brian Aherne Marion Davies	
Dec. 6, 1937	*These Three*	Barbara Stanwyck Errol Flynn Mary Astor	
Dec. 13, 1937	*The Thirty-nine Steps*	Robert Montgomery Ida Lupino	
Dec. 20, 1937	*The Song of Songs*	Marlene Dietrich Douglas Fairbanks, Jr.	
Dec. 27, 1937	*Beloved Enemy*	Madeleine Carroll Brian Aherne	
Jan. 3, 1938	*Alice Adams*	Claudette Colbert Fred MacMurray	
Jan. 10, 1938	*Enter Madame*	Grace Moore Basil Rathbone	
Jan. 17, 1938	*Disraeli*	George Arliss Florence Arliss Pat Patterson	
Jan. 24, 1938	*Clarence*	Bob Burns Gail Patrick	
Jan. 31, 1938	*Green Light*	Errol Flynn Olivia deHavilland	
Feb. 7, 1938	*Anna Christie*	Joan Crawford Spencer Tracy	
Feb. 14, 1938	*Brief Moment*	Ginger Rogers Douglas Fairbanks, Jr.	
Feb. 21, 1938	*Romance*	Madeleine Carroll Herbert Marshall	
Feb. 28, 1938	*Forsaking All Others*	Bette Davis Joel McCrea	
March 7, 1938	*Poppy*	W. C. Fields Anne Shirley John Payne	
March 14, 1938	*The Boss*	Edward Arnold Fay Wray	
March 21, 1938	*The Man Who Played God*	George Arliss Florence Arliss	
March 28, 1938	*Naughty Marietta*	Helen Jepson Lawrence Tibbett	
April 4, 1938	*Dark Victory*	Barbara Stanwyck Melvyn Douglas	
April 11, 1938	*Mary Burns, Fugitive*	Miriam Hopkins Henry Fonda	
April 18, 1938	*Mad About Music*	Deanna Durbin Gail Patrick Herbert Marshall	
April 25, 1938	*Dangerous*	Madeleine Carroll Don Ameche	
May 2, 1938	*The Prisoner of Shark Island*	Gary Cooper Fay Wray	
May 9, 1938	*My Man Godfrey*	Carole Lombard William Powell Gail Patrick Mischa Auer	
May 16, 1938	*The Girl from Tenth Avenue*	Loretta Young George Brent	
May 23, 1938	*The Letter*	Merle Oberon Walter Huston Ralph Forbes	
May 30, 1938	*I Met My Love Again*	Joan Bennett Henry Fonda	
June 6, 1938	*A Doll's House*	Joan Crawford Basil Rathbone	
June 13, 1938	*Theodora Goes Wild*	Cary Grant Irene Dunne	
June 20, 1938	*Manslaughter*	Fredric March Florence Eldridge	
June 27, 1938	*Jane Eyre*	Helen Hayes Robert Montgomery	
July 4, 1938	*I Found Stella Parrish*	Herbert Marshall George Brent Constance Bennett	
Sept. 12, 1938	*Spawn of the North*	Dorothy Lamour George Raft Fred MacMurray	
Sept. 19, 1938	*Morning Glory*	Barbara Stanwyck Ralph Bellamy Melvyn Douglas	
Sept. 26, 1938	*Seven Keys to Baldpate*	Jack Benny Mary Livingstone	
Oct. 3, 1938	*Another Dawn*	Madeleine Carroll George Brent Franchot Tone	
Oct. 10, 1938	*Viva Villa*	Wallace Beery Noah Beery Ellen Drew	
Oct. 17, 1938	*Seventh Heaven*	Jean Arthur Don Ameche	
Oct. 24, 1938	*Babbitt*	Edward Arnold Fay Bainter	
Oct. 31, 1938	*That Certain Woman*	Carole Lombard Jeffrey Lynn Basil Rathbone	
Nov. 7, 1938	*Next Time We Love*	Margaret Sullavan Joel McCrea	
Nov. 14, 1938	*The Buccaneer*	Clark Gable Olympe Bradna	
Nov. 21, 1938	*Confession*	Miriam Hopkins Richard Greene	
Nov. 28, 1938	*Interference*	Herbert Marshall Leslie Howard Gail Patrick Mary Astor	
Dec. 5, 1938	*The Princess Comes Across*	Fred MacMurray Madeleine Carroll	
Dec. 12, 1938	*The Scarlet Pimpernel*	Olivia deHavilland Leslie Howard	
Dec. 19, 1938	*Kid Galahad*	Wayne Morris Edward G. Robinson Andrea Leeds Joan Bennett	
Dec. 26, 1938	*Snow White*	Walt Disney	
Jan. 2, 1939	*The Perfect Specimen*	Errol Flynn Joan Blondell	
Jan. 9, 1939	*Mayerling*	William Powell Janet Gaynor	
Jan. 16, 1939	*Front Page Woman*	Paulette Goddard Fred MacMurray	
Jan. 23, 1939	*Cardinal Richelieu*	George Arliss Florence Arliss Cesar Romero	
Jan. 30, 1939	*The Arkansas Traveler*	Bob Burns Fay Bainter Jean Parker	
Feb. 6, 1939	*The Count of Monte Cristo*	Robert Montgomery Josephine Hutchinson	
Feb. 13, 1939	*The Return of Peter Grimm*	Lionel Barrymore Edward Arnold Maureen O'Sullivan	
Feb. 20, 1939	*Stage Door*	Ginger Rogers Rosalind Russell Adolphe Menjou	

Feb. 27, 1939	*Ceiling Zero*	James Cagney Ralph Bellamy Stuart Erwin	
March 6, 1939	*One Way Passage*	William Powell Kay Francis	
March 13, 1939	*So Big*	Barbara Stanwyck Preston Foster	
March 20, 1939	*It Happened One Night*	Claudette Colbert Clark Gable Walter Connolly Roscoe Karns	
March 27, 1939	*A Man's Castle*	Loretta Young Spencer Tracy	
April 3, 1939	*Silver Dollar*	Edward Arnold Anita Louise Marjorie Rambeau	
April 10, 1939	*The Lives of a Bengal Lancer*	Errol Flynn Brian Aherne C. Aubrey Smith Jackie Cooper	
April 17, 1939	*Bullets or Ballots*	Edward G. Robinson Mary Astor Humphrey Bogart Otto Kruger	
April 24, 1939	*Broadway Bill*	Robert Taylor Frances Dee Gail Patrick	
May 1, 1939	*Lady for a Day*	May Robson Warren William Jean Parker Guy Kibbee	
May 8, 1939	*The Life of Emile Zola*	Paul Muni Josephine Hutchinson	
May 15, 1939	*Tovarich*	William Powell Miriam Hopkins C. Henry Gordon	
May 22, 1939	*Angels with Dirty Faces*	James Cagney Pat O'Brien Gloria Dickson	
May 29, 1939	*Only Angels Have Wings*	Cary Grant Jean Arthur Thomas Mitchell Rita Hayworth Richard Barthelmess	
June 5, 1939	*The Prisoner of Zenda*	Ronald Colman Douglas Fairbanks, Jr. Benita Hume C. Aubrey Smith Ralph Forbes	
June 12, 1939	*White Banners*	Fay Bainter Lewis Stone Jackie Cooper	
June 19, 1939	*The Ex-Mrs. Bradford*	William Powell Claudette Colbert John Archer Alice Eden	
June 26, 1939	*Mrs. Moonlight*	Janet Gaynor George Brent	
July 3, 1939	*Bordertown*	Don Ameche Joan Bennett Claire Trevor	
July 10, 1939	*Ruggles of Red Gap*	Charles Laughton Charlie Ruggles ZaSu Pitts	
Sept. 11, 1939	*The Awful Truth*	Cary Grant Claudette Colbert Phyllis Brooks	
Sept. 18, 1939	*Wuthering Heights*	Barbara Stanwyck Brian Aherne Ida Lupino	
Sept. 25, 1939	*She Married Her Boss*	Ginger Rogers George Brent Edith Fellows	
Oct. 2, 1939	*You Can't Take It With You*	Edward Arnold Walter Connolly Fay Wray Robert Cummings	
Oct. 9, 1939	*The Sisters*	Irene Dunne David Niven	
Oct. 16, 1939	*If I Were King*	Douglas Fairbanks, Jr. Frances Dee Sir Cedric Hardwicke	
Oct. 23, 1939	*Invitation to Happiness*	Fred MacMurray Madeleine Carroll	
Oct. 30, 1939	*The Old Maid*	Loretta Young Miriam Hopkins	
Nov. 6, 1939	*Only Yesterday*	Barbara Stanwyck George Brent	
Nov. 13, 1939	*The Champ*	Wallace Beery Josephine Hutchinson	
Nov. 20, 1939	*Goodbye, Mr. Chips*	Laurence Olivier Edna Best	
Nov. 27, 1939	*Pygmalion*	Jean Arthur Brian Aherne	
Dec. 4, 1939	*A Man to Remember*	Bob Burns Anita Louise	
Dec. 11, 1939	*In Name Only*	Carole Lombard Cary Grant Kay Francis	
Dec. 18, 1939	*Four Daughters*	Lola Lane Leota Lane Priscilla Lane Rosemary Lane Jeffrey Lynn	
Dec. 25, 1939	*Pinocchio*	John Garfield	
Jan. 1, 1940	*Sorrell and Son*	Herbert Marshall Karen Morley Richard Carlson	
Jan. 8, 1940	*Dark Victory*	Bette Davis Spencer Tracy	
Jan. 15, 1940	*Sing You Sinners*	Bing Crosby Ralph Bellamy Jacqueline Wells (Julie Bishop) Elizabeth Patterson	
Jan. 22, 1940	*Bachelor Mother*	Ginger Rogers Fredric March	
Jan. 29, 1940	*Intermezzo*	Herbert Marshall Ingrid Bergman Gail Patrick	
Feb. 5, 1940	*The Young in Heart*	May Robson Don Ameche Ida Lupino Helen Wood	
Feb. 12, 1940	*The Sidewalks of London*	Charles Laughton Elsa Lanchester Alan Marshal	
Feb. 19, 1940	*Made for Each Other*	Carole Lombard Fred MacMurray	
Feb. 26, 1940	*Swing High, Swing Low*	Rudy Vallee Virginia Bruce Una Merkel Roscoe Karns	
March 4, 1940	*Trade Winds*	Joan Bennett Errol Flynn Mary Astor Ralph Bellamy	
March 11, 1940	*My Son, My Son*	Brian Aherne Madeleine Carroll Louis Hayward Josephine Hutchinson	
March 18, 1940	*The Rains Came*	George Brent Kay Francis	
March 25, 1940	*Remember the Night*	Fred MacMurray Barbara Stanwyck Beulah Bondi	

Date	Title	Cast
April 1, 1940	*Love Affair*	Irene Dunne William Powell
April 8, 1940	*Mama Loves Papa*	Fibber McGee Molly
April 15, 1940	*The Underpup*	Gloria Jean Nan Grey Robert Cummings C. Aubrey Smith Beulah Bondi
April 22, 1940	*Abe Lincoln in Illinois*	Raymond Massey Fay Bainter Otto Kruger
April 29, 1940	*Smilin' Through*	Robert Taylor Barbara Stanwyck
May 6, 1940	*Our Town*	William Holden Martha Scott Fay Bainter Beulah Bondi Thomas Mitchell Guy Kibbee Stuart Erwin Frank Craven
May 13, 1940	*True Confession*	Loretta Young Fred MacMurray
May 20, 1940	*Midnight*	Claudette Colbert Don Ameche
May 27, 1940	*Vigil in the Night*	Olivia deHavilland Herbert Marshall Helen Chandler
June 3, 1940	*Alexander's Ragtime Band*	Alice Faye Ray Milland Robert Preston
June 10, 1940	*Till We Meet Again*	Merle Oberon George Brent Pat O'Brien
June 17, 1940	*After the Thin Man*	William Powell Myrna Loy
June 24, 1940	*Show Boat*	Irene Dunne Allan Jones Charles Winninger
July 1, 1940	*Alias the Deacon*	Bob Burns Helen Wood
July 8, 1940	*To the Ladies*	Helen Hayes Otto Kruger
Sept. 9, 1940	*Manhattan Melodrama*	William Powell Myrna Loy Don Ameche
Sept. 16, 1940	*Love Is News*	Bob Hope Madeleine Carroll Ralph Bellamy
Sept. 23, 1940	*The Westerner*	Gary Cooper Doris Davenport Walter Brennan
Sept. 30, 1940	*His Girl Friday*	Claudette Colbert Fred MacMurray
Oct. 7, 1940	*Wings of the Navy*	George Brent Olivia deHavilland John Payne
Oct. 14, 1940	*The Littlest Rebel*	Shirley Temple Claude Rains Preston Foster
Oct. 21, 1940	*Lillian Russell*	Alice Faye Edward Arnold Victor Mature
Oct. 28, 1940	*Strike Up the Band*	Mickey Rooney Judy Garland John Scott Trotter
Nov. 4, 1940	*Wuthering Heights*	Ida Lupino Basil Rathbone
Nov. 11, 1940	*Nothing Sacred*	Douglas Fairbanks, Jr. Joan Bennett
Nov. 18, 1940	*The Rage of Manhattan*	Tyrone Power Annabella
Nov. 25, 1940	*Jezebel*	Loretta Young Brian Donlevy Jeffrey Lynn
Dec. 2, 1940	*Knute Rockne*	Pat O'Brien Fay Wray Donald Crisp Ronald Reagan
Dec. 9, 1940	*My Favorite Wife*	Laurence Olivier Rosalind Russell Gail Patrick
Dec. 16, 1940	*Fifth Avenue Girl*	Ginger Rogers Edward Arnold John Howard
Dec. 23, 1940	*Young Tom Edison*	Mickey Rooney Beulah Bondi Virginia Weidler
Dec. 30, 1940	*A Little Bit of Heaven*	Gloria Jean C. Aubrey Smith Frank Albertson Helen Parrish
Jan. 6, 1941	*Vivacious Lady*	Alice Faye Don Ameche
Jan. 13, 1941	*Libel!*	Ronald Colman Frances Robinson Otto Kruger
Jan. 20, 1941	*The Cowboy and the Lady*	Gene Autry Merle Oberon
Jan. 27, 1941	*Captain January*	Shirley Temple Gene Lockhart Charles Winninger
Feb. 3, 1941	*Rebecca*	Ronald Colman Ida Lupino
Feb. 10, 1941	*The Moon's Our Home*	Carole Lombard James Stewart
Feb. 17, 1941	*Johnny Apollo*	Burgess Meredith Edward Arnold Dorothy Lamour
Feb. 24, 1941	*The Whole Town's Talking*	Fibber McGee Molly
March 3, 1941	*My Bill*	Kay Francis Warren William
March 10, 1941	*The Awful Truth*	Bob Hope Constance Bennett Ralph Bellamy
March 17, 1941	*Cheers for Miss Bishop*	Martha Scott William Gargan
March 24, 1941	*Flight Command*	Robert Taylor Walter Pidgeon Ruth Hussey
March 31, 1941	*Stablemates*	Mickey Rooney Wallace Beery Fay Wray
April 7, 1941	*Stand-In*	Warner Baxter Joan Bennett
April 14, 1941	*Dust Be My Destiny*	John Garfield Claire Trevor
April 21, 1941	*The Letter*	Bette Davis Herbert Marshall James Stephenson
April 28, 1941	*Wife, Husband and Friend*	George Brent Priscilla Lane Gail Patrick
May 5, 1941	*Kitty Foyle*	Ginger Rogers Dennis Morgan James Craig
May 12, 1941	*Craig's Wife*	Rosalind Russell Herbert Marshall
May 19, 1941	*Model Wife*	Dick Powell Joan Blondell
May 26, 1941	*Virginia City*	Errol Flynn Martha Scott

June 2, 1941	*They Drive by Night*	George Raft Lana Turner Lucille Ball	
June 9, 1941	*Mr. and Mrs. Smith*	Bob Hope Carole Lombard	
June 16, 1941	*The Lady from Cheyenne*	Loretta Young Robert Preston Edward Arnold	
June 23, 1941	*The Shop Around the Corner*	Claudette Colbert Don Ameche	
June 30, 1941	*I Love You Again*	Cary Grant Myrna Loy Frank McHugh	
July 7, 1941	*Algiers*	Charles Boyer Hedy Lamarr	
Sept. 8, 1941	*Tom, Dick and Harry*	Ginger Rogers George Murphy Alan Marshal Burgess Meredith	
Sept. 15, 1941	*Lost Horizon*	Ronald Colman Donald Crisp Lynne Carver	
Sept. 22, 1941	*Lydia*	Merle Oberon Edna Mae Oliver Alan Marshal	
Sept. 29, 1941	*Third Finger, Left Hand*	Martha Scott Douglas Fairbanks, Jr.	
Oct. 6, 1941	*Unfinished Business*	Irene Dunne Don Ameche	
Oct. 13, 1941	*Buck Privates*	Bud Abbott Lou Costello	
Oct. 20, 1941	*Blood and Sand*	Tyrone Power Annabella	
Oct. 27, 1941	*Her First Beau*	Jackie Cooper Jane Withers	
Nov. 3, 1941	*Hired Wife*	William Powell Myrna Loy	
Nov. 10, 1941	*Hold Back the Dawn*	Charles Boyer Paulette Goddard Susan Hayward	
Nov. 17, 1941	*Merton of the Movies*	Mickey Rooney Judy Garland	
Nov. 24, 1941	*Maisie Was a Lady*	Ann Sothern Lew Ayres Maureen O'Sullivan Henry Stephenson	
Dec. 1, 1941	*A Man's Castle*	Spencer Tracy Ingrid Bergman	
Dec. 8, 1941	*The Doctor Takes a Wife*	Melvyn Douglas Virginia Bruce	
Dec. 15, 1941	*All This and Heaven Too*	Charles Boyer Bette Davis	
Dec. 22, 1941	*Remember the Night*	Fred MacMurray Jean Arthur	
Dec. 29, 1941	*The Bride Came C.O.D.*	Bob Hope Hedy Lamarr	
Jan. 5, 1942	*Smilin' Through*	Jeanette MacDonald Gene Raymond Brian Aherne	
Jan. 12, 1942	*A Tale of Two Cities*	Ronald Colman Edna Best	
Jan. 19, 1942	*The Devil and Miss Jones*	Lionel Barrymore Lana Turner	
Jan. 26, 1942	*Here Comes Mr. Jordan*	Cary Grant Claude Rains Evelyn Keyes James Gleason	
Feb. 2, 1942	*Skylark*	Claudette Colbert Ray Milland Brian Aherne	
Feb. 9, 1942	*City for Conquest*	Alice Faye Robert Preston	
Feb. 16, 1942	*Blossoms in the Dust*	Greer Garson Walter Pidgeon	
Feb. 23, 1942	*Appointment for Love*	Myrna Loy Charles Boyer	
March 2, 1942	*The Great Lie*	Loretta Young Mary Astor George Brent	
March 9, 1942	*The Lady Eve*	Barbara Stanwyck Ray Milland Charles Coburn	
March 16, 1942	*Manpower*	Marlene Dietrich Edward G. Robinson George Raft	
March 23, 1942	*Strawberry Blonde*	Don Ameche Rita Hayworth Gail Patrick	
March 30, 1942	*I Wanted Wings*	Ray Milland William Holden Veronica Lake	
April 6, 1942	*The Fighting 69th*	Pat O'Brien Robert Preston Ralph Bellamy	
April 13, 1942	*North West Mounted Police*	Gary Cooper Paulette Goddard Preston Foster	
April 20, 1942	*One Foot in Heaven*	Fredric March Martha Scott	
April 27, 1942	*Penny Serenade*	Robert Taylor Barbara Stanwyck Beulah Bondi Edgar Buchanan	
May 4, 1942	*Suspicion*	Joan Fontaine Brian Aherne Nigel Bruce	
May 11, 1942	*The Last of Mrs. Cheyney*	Norma Shearer Walter Pidgeon Adolphe Menjou	
May 18, 1942	*A Man to Remember*	Lionel Barrymore Anita Louise Glenn Ford	
May 25, 1942	*Test Pilot*	Robert Taylor Rita Hayworth Robert Preston	
June 1, 1942	*Ball of Fire*	Barbara Stanwyck Fred MacMurray	
June 8, 1942	*Arise My Love*	Loretta Young Ray Milland	
June 15, 1942	*You Belong to Me*	Merle Oberon George Brent	
June 22, 1942	*Bedtime Story*	Loretta Young Don Ameche	
June 29, 1942	*The Champ*	Wallace Beery Josephine Hutchinson Noah Beery Bobbie Larson	
July 6, 1942	*Love Affair*	Charles Boyer Irene Dunne	
July 13, 1942	*H. M. Pulham, Esquire*	Hedy Lamarr Robert Young Josephine Hutchinson	
July 20, 1942	*The Philadelphia Story* (Victory Show for Government)	Cary Grant Katharine Hepburn Lt. James Stewart Ruth Hussey Virginia Weidler	
Sept. 14, 1942	*This Above All*	Tyrone Power Barbara Stanwyck	
Sept. 21, 1942	*How Green Was My Valley*	Walter Pidgeon Donald Crisp Maureen O'Hara Roddy MacDowall Sara Allgood	

Sept. 28, 1942	*The Magnificent Dope*	Don Ameche Henry Fonda Lynn Bari		April 5, 1943	*The Road to Morocco*	Bing Crosby Bob Hope Ginny Simms
Oct. 5, 1942	*Love Crazy*	William Powell Hedy Lamarr		April 12, 1943	*Once Upon a Honeymoon*	Claudette Colbert Brian Aherne Laird Cregar Albert Dekker
Oct. 12, 1942	*Morning Glory*	Judy Garland John Payne Adolphe Menjou		April 19, 1943	*A Night to Remember*	Ann Sothern Robert Young
Oct. 19, 1942	*My Favorite Blonde*	Bob Hope Virginia Bruce		April 26, 1943	*The Lady Has Plans*	William Powell Rita Hayworth
Oct. 26, 1942	*Wake Island*	Brian Donlevy Robert Preston Broderick Crawford		May 3, 1943	*The Navy Comes Through*	Pat O'Brien Ruth Hussey George Murphy
Nov. 2, 1942	*A Woman's Face*	Ida Lupino Brian Aherne Conrad Veidt		May 10, 1943	*Now, Voyager*	Ida Lupino Paul Henreid Dame Mae Whitty Albert Dekker
Nov. 9, 1942	*Sullivan's Travels*	Veronica Lake Ralph Bellamy		May 17, 1943	*The Talk of the Town*	Ronald Colman Cary Grant Jean Arthur
Nov. 16, 1942	*To Mary with Love*	Irene Dunne Ray Milland Otto Kruger		May 24, 1943	*Hitler's Children*	Bonita Granville Otto Kruger Kent Smith Walter Reed
Nov. 23, 1942	*The Gay Sisters*	Barbara Stanwyck Robert Young		May 31, 1943	*The Major and the Minor*	Ginger Rogers Ray Milland Mrs. Lela Rogers
Nov. 30, 1942	*Broadway*	George Raft Lloyd Nolan Janet Blair		June 7, 1943	*My Friend Flicka*	Roddy MacDowall George Brent Rita Johnson
Dec. 7, 1942	*The War Against Mrs. Hadley*	Fay Bainter Edward Arnold Jean Rogers Van Johnson		June 14, 1943	*The Philadelphia Story*	Robert Taylor Loretta Young Robert Young
Dec. 14, 1942	*Algiers*	Charles Boyer Loretta Young		June 21, 1943	*In Which We Serve*	Ronald Colman Edna Best
Dec. 21, 1942	*The Pied Piper*	Frank Morgan Ralph Morgan Anne Baxter Roddy McDowall		June 28, 1943	*The Great Man's Lady*	Barbara Stanwyck Joseph Cotten Chester Morris
Dec. 28, 1942	*A Star Is Born*	Judy Garland Walter Pidgeon		July 5, 1943	*My Sister Eileen*	Rosalind Russell Brian Aherne Janet Blair
Jan. 4, 1943	*The Bugle Sounds*	Wallace Beery Marjorie Rambeau Noah Beery		July 12, 1943	*Air Force*	George Raft Harry Carey
Jan. 11, 1943	*She Knew All the Answers*	Joan Bennett Preston Foster Eve Arden		Sept. 13, 1943	*The Phantom of the Opera*	Nelson Eddy Susanna Foster Basil Rathbone
Jan. 18, 1943	*My Gal Sal*	Mary Martin Dick Powell		Sept. 20, 1943	*Flight for Freedom*	Rosalind Russell George Brent Chester Morris
Jan. 25, 1943	*This Gun for Hire*	Joan Blondell Laird Cregar Alan Ladd		Sept. 27, 1943	*Ladies in Retirement*	Ida Lupino Brian Aherne Dame May Whitty Edith Barrett
Feb. 1, 1943	*The Show-Off*	Harold Peary Una Merkel Beulah Bondi		Oct. 4, 1943	*The Pride of the Yankees*	Gary Cooper Virginia Bruce Edgar Buchanan
Feb. 8, 1943	*The Maltese Falcon*	Edward G. Robinson Gail Patrick Laird Cregar		Oct. 11, 1943	*Heaven Can Wait*	Don Ameche Maureen O'Hara
Feb. 15, 1943	*Are Husbands Necessary?*	George Burns Gracie Allen		Oct. 18, 1943	*Mr. Lucky*	Cary Grant Laraine Day
Feb. 22, 1943	*This Is the Army*	All-Soldier Cast		Oct. 25, 1943	*Slightly Dangerous*	Lana Turner Victor Mature Gene Lockhart
March 1, 1943	*The Lady Is Willing*	Kay Francis George Brent				
March 8, 1943	*Reap the Wild Wind*	Paulette Goddard Ray Milland John Carradine		Nov. 1, 1943	*So Proudly We Hail*	Claudette Colbert Veronica Lake Paulette Goddard Sonny Tufts Les Tremayne
March 15, 1943	*Libel!*	Edna Best Ronald Colman Otto Kruger		Nov. 8, 1943	*Salute to the Marines*	Wallace Beery Fay Bainter Noah Beery
March 22, 1943	*Each Dawn I Die*	George Raft Franchot Tone Lynn Bari				
March 29, 1943	*Crossroads*	Lana Turner Jean Pierre Aumont		Nov. 15, 1943	*Hello, Frisco, Hello*	Alice Faye Robert Young

Nov. 22, 1943	*China*	Loretta Young Alan Ladd William Bendix	
Nov. 29, 1943	*The Navy Comes Through*	Pat O'Brien Ruth Warrick Chester Morris	
Dec. 6, 1943	*Mrs. Miniver*	Greer Garson Walter Pidgeon Susan Peters Ensign Henry Wilcoxon	
Dec. 13, 1943	*Five Graves to Cairo*	Franchot Tone Anne Baxter Otto Preminger J. Carroll Naish Fortunio Bonanova	

May 1, 1944	*Appointment for Love*	Paul Lukas Olivia deHavilland
May 8, 1944	*Penny Serenade*	Irene Dunne Joseph Cotten Edgar Buchanan
May 15, 1944	*Action in the North Atlantic*	George Raft Raymond Massey Julie Bishop
May 22, 1944	*Springtime in the Rockies*	Betty Grable Dick Powell Carmen Miranda Edgar Barrier

Dec. 20, 1943 — *Dixie* — Bing Crosby, Dorothy Lamour, Barry Sullivan

May 29, 1944 — *Old Acquaintance* — Alexis Smith, Miriam Hopkins, Otto Kruger

Dec. 27, 1943 — *Kathleen* — Shirley Temple, Herbert Marshall, Frances Gifford

June 5, 1944 — *Jane Eyre* — Orson Welles, Loretta Young

Jan. 3, 1944 — *Shadow of a Doubt* — William Powell, Teresa Wright

June 12, 1944 — *Naughty Marietta* — Nelson Eddy, Jeanette MacDonald

Jan. 10, 1944 — *The Constant Nymph* — Charles Boyer, Alexis Smith, Maureen O'Sullivan

June 19, 1944 — *Lost Angel* — Margaret O'Brien, James Craig, Marsha Hunt, Keenan Wynn

Jan. 17, 1944 — (No Show—Gov't. Pre-empt)

June 26, 1944 — *Christmas in July* — Dick Powell, Linda Darnell, Raymond Walburn

Jan. 24, 1944 — *Casablanca* — Hedy Lamarr, John Loder, Alan Ladd, Edgar Barrier

July 3, 1944 — *It Happened Tomorrow* — Don Ameche, Anne Baxter

Sept. 4, 1944 — *Maytime* — Nelson Eddy, Jeanette MacDonald, Edgar Barrier

Jan. 31, 1944 — *Random Harvest* — Greer Garson, Ronald Colman

Feb. 7, 1944 — *His Butler's Sister* — Deanna Durbin, Pat O'Brien, Robert Paige

Sept. 11, 1944 — *Break of Hearts* — Orson Welles, Rita Hayworth

Feb. 14, 1944 — *The Fallen Sparrow* — Robert Young, Maureen O'Hara, Walter Slezak

Sept. 18, 1944 — *Suspicion* — William Powell, Olivia deHavilland

Sept. 25, 1944 — *Lucky Partners* — Don Ameche, Lucille Ball

Feb. 21, 1944 — *Wake Up and Live* — Frank Sinatra, Bob Crosby, Jimmy Gleason, Marilyn Maxwell, James Dunn

Oct. 2, 1944 — *Home in Indiana* — Walter Brennan, Charlotte Greenwood, Edward Ryan, Jeanne Crain, June Haver

Feb. 28, 1944 — *Guadalcanal Diary* — Preston Foster, William Bendix, Lloyd Nolan, Richard Jaeckel

Oct. 9, 1944 — *In Old Chicago* — Dorothy Lamour, Robert Young, John Hodiak

March 6, 1944 — *The Letter* — Bette Davis, Herbert Marshall, Vincent Price

Oct. 16, 1944 — *Seventh Heaven* — Van Johnson, Jennifer Jones, Jean Hersholt, Billy Gilbert

March 13, 1944 — *In Old Oklahoma* — Roy Rogers, Martha Scott, Albert Dekker

Oct. 23, 1944 — *The Story of Dr. Wassell* — Gary Cooper, Barbara Britton, Carol Thurston

March 20, 1944 — *The Hard Way* — Miriam Hopkins, Franchot Tone, Anne Baxter, Chester Morris

Oct. 30, 1944 — *Standing Room Only* — Paulette Goddard, Fred MacMurray

Nov. 6, 1944 — *The Pied Piper* — Frank Morgan, Margaret O'Brien, Signe Hasso

March 27, 1944 — *The Phantom Lady* — Brian Aherne, Ella Raines, Alan Curtis

Nov. 13, 1944 — *Magnificent Obsession* — Claudette Colbert, Don Ameche

April 3, 1944 — *Destroyer* — Edward G. Robinson, Marguerite Chapman, Dennis O'Keefe

Nov. 20, 1944 — *It Started with Eve* — Charles Laughton, Dick Powell, Susanna Foster

April 10, 1944 — *The Happy Land* — Don Ameche, Frances Dee, Walter Brennan

Nov. 27, 1944 — *Dark Waters* — Merle Oberon, Preston Foster, Thomas Mitchell

April 17, 1944 — *Coney Island* — Alan Ladd, Dorothy Lamour, Chester Morris

Dec. 4, 1944 — *The Unguarded Hour* — Robert Montgomery, Laraine Day, Roland Young

April 24, 1944 — *This Land Is Mine* — Charles Laughton, Maureen O'Sullivan, Edgar Barrier

Dec. 11, 1944 — *Casanova Brown* — Gary Cooper, Joan Bennett, Thomas Mitchell

Dec. 18, 1944	*Berkeley Square*	Ronald Colman Maureen O'Sullivan	Jan. 15, 1945	*The Master Race*	Paul Guilfoyle George Coulouris Nancy Gates Stanley Ridges Helen Beverly
Dec. 25, 1944	*The Vagabond King*	Dennis Morgan Kathryn Grayson J. Carroll Naish			
Jan. 1, 1945	*Bride by Mistake*	Laraine Day John Hodiak Marsha Hunt	Jan. 22, 1945	*Tender Comrade*	Olivia deHavilland June Duprez Dennis O'Keefe
Jan. 8, 1945	*I Never Left Home*	Bob Hope Frances Langford Jerry Colonna Tony Romano			